What People are Saying:

*Howard Strickland has the heart of a pastor.
His love for people comes through convincingly
and colorfully in his new release, <u>Text Messages
From God</u>. He blends the old and the new in
practical stories and truths that stimulate the
soul and challenges the mind to think positively
and creatively.*

*The timely and scriptural messages will guide
you on a thrilling journey of Rejecting
Negativism, Walking in Increase, Living In The
Moment and other subjects that will add depth
and sparkle to your walk with the Lord and
testimony.*

> Raymond F. Culpepper, D.D.
> General Overseer of Church of
> God International Offices
> Cleveland, Tennessee

*Howard Strickland has done the Kingdom a great
service by writing TEXT MESSAGES FROM GOD.
Seizing the contemporary model of cell phone text
messaging,*

*Doctor Strickland lays out a Biblical model for
discovering one's purpose and moving on that God given
assignment. This book will encourage all who read it on
their life's journey. All believers can profit from this fine
book.*

> Dr. Ron Phillips
> Abba's House at Central Baptist Church
> Chattanooga, Tennessee

I am so impressed with Dr. Strickland's new book "Text Messages from God". A lot of time and anointing went into the writing of this book. I love the chapter "Rejecting Negativism", especially the part that says... whatever you do in life don't be afraid of failure. For 35 years, I have said "Failure is not final with the Father."

The North Carolina College of Theology has over 1000 students graduate each year, with a Bible degree. We hope next year, that we can require all our students to write their dissertation on this wonderful book .

Dr. Strickland, I'm so proud of you!

Dr. J.L. Cook, Ph.D.
President & Founder
North Carolina College of Theology

My friend of more than twenty years, Howard Strickland, has written a thought provoking book as indicated by the title, "Text Messages From God."
He shows us the ultimate purpose of God for mankind is the responsibility of a return to stewardship. Most people think that freedom means a license to do whatever they please without any accountability.
The author brings us back to the realization that freedom comes with a price tag.

Dr. Joe E Edwards
The Church at Liberty Square
Cartersville, Ga

Text Messages From God

Practical Messages That Touch The Heart

Discover Your Purpose and Assignment For Life!

Purchase at www.amazon.com or
www.howardstrickland.com

Howard A. Strickland, TH.D

Text Messages From God

Copyright © 2009 Howard A. Strickland

ISBN: 1442131020

Acknowledgments

I would like to thank my Lord, Savior and King for everything He does!

Yet in all these things we are more than conquerors through Him who loved us.
Romans 8:37

I also want to thank my wife for helping with this book. She has read, spell-checked, and so much more. My wife is such an encourager! Jenny never complains. For over twenty-two years she has allowed Christ to have first place in my life. Sometimes she has to wait, but she does not whine or grumble. Instead, Jenny prays for me so I will hear the inner voice. I love you Jenny Strickland. You will be rewarded.

I am so proud of my two boys Nathan and Daniel, who have decided to follow the God of their parents and now know Him personally. Jenny and I are truly blessed. Furthermore, I would like to thank my son Nathan for designing and creating the front cover of this book.

Many thanks to Dad and Mom for praying for me, back when. I could not have better parents. And what an example they provided: over 60 years of marriage!

Much gratitude to my mother-in-law Mary, who always prays for me, and speaks the truth lovingly.

Crane Eater Community Church. A people of Love, Prayer and Grace. Together we shall be fruitful.

Bible Versions Used and Their Abbreviations

The New King James Bible is the primary translation used throughout this book. If no abbreviation follows a quotation of scripture, you may assume it is from the New King James Bible. Other translations are sometimes used, and are abbreviated as follows:

King James/ KJ

Amplified Bible/ Amp

New Living Translation/ NLT

The Message Bible/ TM

New International Version/ NIV

All versions of the Bible are used with written permission.

Table of Contents

Man's Greatest Need

In the meantime His disciples urged Him, saying, "Rabbi, eat." But He said to them, "I have food to eat of which you do not know." Therefore the disciples said to one another, "Has anyone brought Him anything to eat?" Jesus said to them, "My food is to do the will of Him who sent Me, and to finish His work. Do you not say, 'There are still four months and then comes the harvest'? Behold, I say to you, lift up your eyes and look at the fields, for they are already white for harvest!
(John 4: 31-35)

Jesus has always been moved by the sin and sorrow of mankind. Thus, the cry of His heart surpassed His physical sensations and appetites. His meat was to fill the emptiness of every human heart. Jesus was sent by the Father to save humanity. The perfect Son of God came down and became flesh and dwelt among man. Isn't that amazing?

And the Word became flesh and dwelt among us, and we beheld His glory, the glory as of the only begotten of the Father, full of grace and truth. (John 1:14)

The greatest need in the world is for all mankind to be saved, healed, and delivered from sin. Individuals impair their priorities when the cares of the world are allowed to enter in before they dialogue with God. That's why it's important believers take time and allow Christ to direct their steps.

The steps of a good man are ordered by the Lord, and He delights in his way. (Psalm 37:23)

God longs to order the steps of righteous men and women. When Jesus does not have precedence within His creation their minds becomes inundated with the things of this world. Cosmos dominates; however, that has never been the creator's intention. God personally invested Himself in every person. He breathed His life within mankind so man in return would fellowship with Him. He covets fellowship with you.

Listen to this prayer by - St Patrick- It's called the "Lorica"- named for a Roman coat of armor that is meant for the protection <u>of the one wearing it</u>:

> I arise today Through a mighty strength, the invocation of the Trinity, Through a belief in the Threeness, Through confession of the Oneness Of the Creator of creation.
>
> I arise today Through the strength of Christ's birth and His baptism, Through the strength of His crucifixion and His burial, Through the strength of His resurrection and His ascension, Through the strength of His descent for the judgment of doom.
>
> I arise today Through the strength of the love of cherubim, In obedience of angels, In service of archangels, In the hope of resurrection to meet with reward, In the prayers of patriarchs, In preachings of the apostles,

3

In faiths of confessors, In innocence of virgins, In deeds of righteous men.

I arise today through the strength of Heaven the rays of the sun, the radiance of the moon, the splendor of fire, the speed of lightening, the swiftness of the wind, the depth of the sea, the stability of the earth the firmness of rock.

I arise today through the power of God: God's might to comfort me, God's wisdom to guide me, God's eye to look before me, God's ear to hear me, God's word to speak for me, God's hand to lead me, God's way to lie before me, God's shield to protect me, God's Heavenly Host to save me from the snares of the devil, from temptations to sin, from all who wish me ill, from near and afar, alone and with others.

May Christ shield me today against poison and fire, against drowning and wounding, so that I may fulfill my mission and bear fruit in abundance.

Christ behind and before me, Christ

behind and above me, Christ with me and in me, Christ around and about me, Christ on my right and on my left, Christ when I lie down at night, Christ when I rise in the morning, Christ in the heart of every man who thinks of me, Christ in the mouth of everyone that speaks of me, Christ in every eye that sees me, Christ in every ear that hears me. [1]

Jesus Christ desires fellowship; His passion is to dine with you. Think about this, Eating with the King daily. Partaking from the Creators table. No leftovers, or warmed over, half baked food. A serving straight from the Masters heavenly bakery.

Do not love the world or the things in the world. If anyone loves the world, the love of the Father is not in him. For all that is in the world—the lust of the flesh, the lust of the eyes, and the pride of life—is not of the Father but is of the world. And the world is passing away, and the lust of it; but he who does the will of God abides forever.
(I John 2:15-17)

Jesus' disciples were caught up in thinking only of Jesus' physical needs. Jesus' need to fulfill the will of His Father was not <u>their first priority</u>. In I John 2, these verses give you the three deadly sins:

- ✤ <u>The lust of the flesh</u>
- ✤ <u>The lust of the eye</u>
- ✤ <u>The pride of life</u>

Jesus' disciples were thinking carnal. They were good men but carnal men; however, the Son of God had a Master plan prepared.

Our priorities are important to God. He designed you to seek Him first.

As the deer longs for streams of water, so I long for you, O God. (Psalm 42:1 NLT)

Healing serves no purpose without salvation. Miracles have no meaning, money is vanity, life is dark, the grave has the final say and mankind is lost without Jesus Christ. Jesus said, *I have food to eat of which you do not know.* The Father has given His Son revelation.

Once the present is unveiled, the future can be manifested. Time, love, and passion are required for all who desire to eat Spiritual food. Jesus never intended to keep anything from His children.

God doesn't play games with you; He doesn't laugh at your expense. It has always been His desire to give you insight. God said to his prophet Jeremiah (33:3), *Call to Me, and I will answer you, and show you great and mighty things which you do not know.*

This word came to Jeremiah as he was locked away for doing God's will. As strange as it might seem, when you listen and become aware of Him, it has the potential of becoming the greatest thing you could possibly do. Moreover, these kinds of moments, can change the spiritual season in your life, and propel you into greater destiny. Everyone hungers for that.

In John's gospel, we see that Jesus loved the woman who had five husbands. Now, she's shacking up. Doesn't it make sense that He loves you too? While you were still a sinner,

Christ died for you. Surely He loves you right now as His sons and His daughters.

> *So you have not received a spirit that makes you fearful slaves. Instead, you received God's Spirit when he adopted you as his own children. Now we call him, "Abba, Father." For his Spirit joins with our spirit to affirm that we are God's children. And since we are his children, we are his heirs. In fact, together with Christ we are heirs of God's glory. But if we are to share his glory, we must also share his suffering.* (Romans 8:15-17 NLT)

One of the biggest tricks of the enemy is to scam us and deceive us into thinking that salvation is earned by merit. But what Jesus Christ did on the cross finished all work. Moreover, for every believer, He suppressed the mouth of condemnation for eternity.

> *There is therefore now no condemnation to those who are in Christ Jesus, who do not walk according to the flesh, but according to the Spirit.* (Romans 8:1)

If you are a Christian, you are one of His

people. You heard His call while living in total darkness. Your mouth ought to be filled with praise. You have eaten from His table. You have tasted His delights.

> *But you are a chosen generation, a royal priesthood, a holy nation, His own special people, that you may proclaim the praises of Him who called you out of darkness into His marvelous light; who once were not a people but are now the people of God, who had not obtained mercy but now have obtained mercy.*
> (I Peter 2:9-10)

You are able to go from strangers to being His chosen, from no mercy, to full mercy. What a trade. That's what I call a great exchange!

> *"But Jesus needed to go through Samaria."*
> (John 4:4)

What a wonderful Savior, Jesus left a revival in Judaea for **one** Samaritan woman.

Imagine, Jesus having needs. So what are His needs?

First, He wants you to receive salvation, and to get you heaven ready.

Let not your heart be troubled; you believe in God, believe also in Me. In My Father's house are many mansions; if it were not so, I would have told you. I go to prepare a place for you. (John 14:1-2)

Secondly, He wants you to have purpose, and direction.

For I know the thoughts that I think toward you, says the LORD, thoughts of peace and not of evil, to give you a future and a hope.

(Jeremiah 29:11)

Thirdly, He desires to instill greatness within you.

You are of God, little children, and have overcome them, because He who is in you is greater than he who is in the world.
(I John 4:4)

Jesus has placed His seed of greatness within you, so let it grow.

In Jesus' era, no righteous Jews traveled through Samaria (called Sychar) because it represented falsehood and drunkenness. It was known as a city of reproach.[2] However, traveling through Samaria made Jesus' journey three days shorter. But the real reason Jesus traveled through this town was because of a divine stirring to help lost souls. Jesus' meat was to do His Father's will; therefore, His meat became His mission. He forever lives to help each and every person.

In the natural realm, nothing stimulates, keeps alive, or maintains courage more than seeing success in the mission one is dedicated to live out daily. So what is your need? If you are a driver, factory worker, a sales person, or a CEO- become Christ-driven. Christ died for a mission, and His ultimate mission became you. As you allow Christ to order your steps, you will find purpose, and direction like you have never experienced before.

> *In the meantime His disciples urged Him,*
> *saying, "Rabbi, eat."*   (John 4:31)

Was Jesus eating? He surely was. He was eating directly from His Father's table. The best meal you will ever eat will come when you do the Father's will. Doing His will brings you into His climate, and His way of doing things. You might even find that it is unconventional, but God's word will never change. However, sometimes the way you approach God's word, and present it *does* change.

Allow your imagination free rein as you turn toward Him. Allow Him to speak to you. Stay prepared to write and act on what He says to you. You can't tell others around you until you act on God's word. Maybe then you can share it with others. Christ desires to position you for change, and then He will propel you to become a voice to others. If you aren't transformed how can you help others? If your motive isn't true, how can you expect God's life changing power to influence others. **Remember this, living skeptical in attitude suggests little more than total loss.**

While growing up in a small town, we attended a great church that had this mission statement: "Doing small things so large things can occur." So I say unto you, "Eat." There is nothing like eating a meal that fills you just right. You get up from the table not too full but just right. Eat from His table and you won't come up empty. You are going to find satisfaction, rest, peace and faith like you have never lived in.

> *Are you tired? Worn out? Burned out on religion? Come to me. Get away with me and you'll recover your life. I'll show you how to take a real rest. Walk with me and work with me—watch how I do it. Learn the unforced rhythms of grace. I won't lay anything heavy or ill-fitting on you. Keep company with me and you'll learn to live freely and lightly.*
> (Matthew 11:28-30 TM)

Many in the body of Christ are hanging by a thread. These people hear about church, or listen to a minister on television and they feel turned off. Why? Because they are not eating from Jesus' table. You can't live by second-hand revelation only. People have to receive first-hand revelation for themselves. Maybe once they did. Now they are just going through the motions. Life isn't about living, and doing what you want to do. Full and wholesome life begins and ends by doing the Father's will.

Thriving, loving, and caring for others teaches you to stay focused. It gives us direction and purpose for life. Most of the time, a person will not feel like seeking God. However, if you will seek Him, He promises to bring new direction and purpose with clarity. You can grow and become alive spiritually, but it takes discipleship. If you're employed by a company, and decided you were not coming into work, and this behavior became your habit, you would be fired sooner rather than later. Your walk with Jesus Christ usually is a good reflection of your work-ethic. Believe it or not, even a person's physical countenance is a reflection to an individual's spiritual walk.

Eat, eat, and eat some more from Jesus' table. You can't go wrong. Please, never feed other people while you are hungry. If you have not eaten the food you give to others, it could be old, and stale because you haven't even tried it yourself. That can become dangerous for you and others. Stale bread is not too appetizing and it will make one malnourished both physically and spiritually. If you are a church member, it is your duty to pray for your pastor. After much prayer, if the manna is still old, cold, and dry you might want to find a new feeding station. However, most of the time, it's not that you need a change. No. Usually you need to personally take responsibility.

I was in a meeting not long ago where any and every minister could speak about their concerns. Most of the pastors who approached the microphone were very critical of the leadership. However, it wasn't the leadership who was at fault. I have found instead of passing the buck, or laying the blame on others, if you take accountability, you will continue to grow even though it hurts.

> *Therefore the disciples said to one another,*
> *"Has anyone brought Him anything to eat?"*
> (John 4:33)

When unbelief is present, isn't it something

how the unfaithful gravitate toward one
another, substituting God in any form? Jesus'
disciples asked the question, "How did He get
food?" As a person leaves their old habits, and
friends there will be some who will try to bring
distractions. People who are negative tend to
run with that certain pack. At school, you can
watch as kids of all ages begin to form small
packs. If you could listen in on those
conversations, you would hear words, or see
smiles of edification or destruction.

*Whoever guards his mouth and tongue keeps
his soul from troubles.* (Proverbs 21:23)

Our words will bring either encouragement
or pain.
Listen to Jesus' response to his disciples:

*Jesus said to them, "My food is to do the will
of Him who sent Me, and to finish His work.*
(John 4:34)

How many of you have driven miles to eat a
good meal? Not long ago, I went with some
friends to a place in the middle of nowhere to

eat. Guess what? It was worth it. One of these days, I will try my best to take my family back there so they can experience the taste. When I began to pastor my first church, there were only seven people in attendance. It really looked impossible for that old, small church to ever grow, but through God's grace, and our willingness to do what He said, it grew and we relocated. Today, that church is thriving.

When you really taste Christ, you will come back for more. Seconds, please. Can you imagine hearing words like that as your pastor preaches? Wow! What if people cried out, **"Let's stay another hour and hear pastor teach and preach some more!"** Jesus is actually saying, that His food primarily begins with the Father's view on any situation. Have you actually stopped to ask the question, "Lord, what do You think about this?" When you accomplish the things in life you were created to do, Christ will be pleased with your goals.

Happy are the people who are in such a state;
Happy are the people whose God is their
LORD!   (Psalm 144:15)

What's your state of mind? While in college, I took a speech class. For the final grade each student chose a subject, and had to communicate the subject in unique ways. I selected happiness. I recorded myself laughing and played it loud. Everyone began to roll with laughter. Then I selected four students to begin laughing together, and the whole class broke up with laughter again.

After that I asked four students who had left the room to enter without looking up. I told them to show emotions of depression and despair. Quickly, everyone in the class began to show those same feelings. What am I saying?

Happiness is addicting. Try it. Happiness is always found within. It's a state-of-mind. You might not like this, but you are responsible for yourself. Going back, Jesus' greatest desire was to please His Father who sent Him so all mankind could be saved. So, what's your state of mind? Pray about it, and allow God to change it. There will be no blaming others on judgment day.

Because of storms and people's opinions, many individuals start to accomplish something while others get blown off course. They start off with real passion only to allow situations to stop them. These obstacles can be removed by having vision and purpose. When a person writes his purpose and plan down on paper, and maybe even hangs it in a familiar place, it will eventually become that person's testimony. The only true reason for doing anything should be to please God. One day He will say, "Well done!" Our church's mission statement is to be "A people of love, prayer and grace." Love everyone. Pray for others. Grace even the unloveable just as Christ Jesus graced you! What if everyone lived by those three rules?

Finally Jesus said:

Do you not say, 'There are still four months and then comes the harvest?' Behold, I say to you, lift up your eyes and look at the fields,

for they are already white for harvest!
(John 4:35)

There are so many means to reach the harvest. Showing a movie on a big screen outside, providing free food, or having a party while the church family serves all the guests lunch. Think outside the box because the harvest is limitless. While many procrastinate and say tomorrow. Jesus cries out, "The harvest is ripe!"

Hebrews 11:1 starts off by saying, "Now faith is...." I do not think it is happenstance that the writer penned, "Now faith." It is important for us to understand that Christ expects us to walk in present and active faith. Harvest-time is a demanding time; all must be then at work. Harvest-time is a short period, and harvest-work must be done now, or not at all. The time of the gospel is a season, and once it passes, you cannot return to it or recall it.

For as long as Earth lasts, planting and harvest, cold and heat, summer and winter,

day and night will never stop.
                    (Genesis 8:22 TM)

There are many who miss their season and most are full of regret. It's time to open your eyes, and look around. **The harvest cannot be reaped from a distance**, so jump in and get busy. Today is the day.

Questions

Can be answered in a group, or as an individual

What moves you?

What is found in your steps?

What is your priority?

What is your divine stirring?

What makes you turn around for another look?

What makes you cry?

How can you make a difference?

What will bring you into your season?

Does church ever turn you off

Do you expect a harvest?

What will a Spiritual harvest look like?

How much time can you invest?

Are you willing to roll your selves up?

Is your primary role to sow or reap?

Do you know your gift or gifts?

Our Assignment

The day you allow Jesus Christ to come and reside within, you became assigned to His mission, His calling, and His way of thinking. God always has a purpose for you. God doesn't function through happenstance, God works through specific goals. God has given you personal assignments. Moreover, He has given us **corporate assignments**.

> *How wonderful and pleasant it is when brothers live together in harmony! For harmony is as precious as the anointing oil that was poured over Aaron's head, that ran down his beard and onto the border of his robe. Harmony is as refreshing as the dew from Mount Hermon that falls on the mountains of Zion. And there the Lord has pronounced his blessing, even life everlasting.* (Psalm 133:1-3 NLT)

Notice, unity flows wherever there are brothers working together. Also, in this atmosphere, God commands blessings of life. Everyone desires a good life now, and life forever, don't they? Sadly not, many suppress and eventually halt unity when child like behavior isn't dealt with.

Many people believe that only bad things happen to them. Almost always the good, or bad can be traced back to the universal law of sowing and reaping. My dad told me when I was younger, "Howard, if you do bad you will get caught up with!" He was right. Paul writing to the early church said this:

> *Do not be deceived: God cannot be mocked. A man reaps what he sows. The one who sows to please his sinful nature, from that nature will reap destruction; the one who sows to please the Spirit, from the Spirit will reap eternal life.* (Galatians 6:7-8 NIV)

For example, if a person eats too much he or she will become overweight, and be subject to health problems. If an individual drives too fast, he or she increases their chance of an accident.

Your assignment was given, and planned out

for you before you were created.

Before I formed you in the womb I knew you;
Before you were born I sanctified you; I
ordained you a prophet to the nations.
(Jeremiah 1:5)

God's ideas for your life are larger than your plans, so hang on to God. Stop looking to other sources, it's not too late—you can still follow God's plan. He's waiting for you to catch up. Remember, God loves you too much to leave you behind.

Now the LORD had said to Abram, "Get out
of your country, from your family and from
your father's house, to a land that I will show
you. I will make you a great nation; I will
bless you and make your name great; and you
shall be a blessing. I will bless those who
bless you, and I will curse him who curses
you; and in you all the families of the earth
shall be blessed. (Genesis 12:1-3)

Think about this reality: no cell phones and no wireless Internet. Nothing. As Abram left he was basically saying goodbye to everyone and everything that was ever near or dear to him. Are you willing to say goodbye to the familiar?

> *Looking unto Jesus, the author and finisher of our faith, who for the joy that was set before Him endured the cross, despising the shame, and has sat down at the right hand of the throne of God.* (Hebrew 12:2)

Sometimes people have a tendency to read these Bible verses as only words in a book, but this was a real man in a real world. He had real emotions, and fears like you have. Be reminded that Jesus Christ underwent every trial you might experience.

> *For we do not have a High Priest who cannot sympathize with our weaknesses, but was in all points tempted as we are, yet without sin. Let us therefore come boldly to the throne of grace, that we may obtain mercy and find grace to help in time of need.*
> (Hebrews 4:15-16)

I'm so happy He is touched by my weaknesses. Imagine Abram's apprehension: no hotels, stores, or restaurants, just barren land. As Abram left, he was completely obedient, and according to Romans chapter 4, his obedience would turn into faith. Real faith does not pull away from God's assignment just because it becomes scary. No, real faith becomes ingrained within you to the point that you might fall, but you understand you have to get back up. After all, you have destiny living within you. You have heard God's call.

I have learned that high level's of obedience brings mountain-moving faith. I think many in the body of Christ are looking to increase their faith. However, the greatest way for this to occur comes through obedience to God. As a person is obedient, God will help their walk, talk, and actions. You are not alone.

> *And I will ask the Father, and He will give you another Comforter (Counselor, Helper, Intercessor, Advocate, Strengthener, and Standby), that He may remain with you forever—*   (John 14:16 Amp)

As you probably know there are many doctrines about faith and one is called Election.

It teaches that only some are called, chosen, and saved. However, another doctrine that comes straight from God's word is this one:

For God so loved the world that He gave His only Son, that whosoever believes in Him shall not perish but have everlasting life. (John 3:16)

I call this doctrine, **"Whosoever."** Whosoever calls on the name of the Lord shall be saved. Now whosoever might not be a real doctrine, however, I believe in whosoever. I am so glad God gives whosoever an assignment. God looks for whosoever. Here's a few examples. Esther was a "whosoever," the woman at the well was a "whosoever," Paul was a "whosoever," and you, my friend, are a "whosoever!"

I believe God gave Adam and Eve an assignment. In Genesis 11, God gave Terah an assignment, but he stopped before he came into his destiny. Therefore, God gives Abram the same task to complete. So Abram left all, and became the father of faith. As you think about these names you can quickly see that very few men and women followed God's assignment. Abraham was successful because of his obedience. Obedience will make you successful, too.

Unfortunately, God's best does not happen for many men. They plan and do their own thing, and go their own way. It's truly amazing that God loves men, and women regardless of their decisions. Just remember, please do not settle for less than God's best.

In Galatians, Paul writes that faith works by love. Just think for a minute, the progression that would have occurred if all these men and women had followed God's assignment instead of their own. The advancement in mankind's knowledge, health, and lives in general would be off the chart. Godliness, joy, peace, and love would fill the atmosphere. If faith is present you can know that God's love is ruling. In return, great leaps of advancement will be made.

Our assignment is not always glamorous.

Just ask someone who has been on the mission field all their life. My mother lead the Ladies Missions group in her church for years. Once she invited a missionary who had lived in China for over thirty years to speak while in America. The missionary had lived and portrayed the life of Christ among the people of China, but after all those years she only led one person to the Lord Jesus Christ! Was she successful? Yes, she was. Her whole life radiated Christ, and when she gets to heaven she will hear the Master say, "Well done!" The times I have experienced the hand of God. I can tell you it wasn't very slick or sensational. No, it was just staying faithful to God's call and walking in love even when it's not fun.

A few years ago, I had the opportunity to go and teach leadership principles to twenty-one pastors in the Ukraine. These men of God were already serving in three to four churches each. They traveled by bicycle from one church to another. Every morning at twelve, the men would break out in prayer for around an hour.

Some of them had traveled a couple hundred miles just to stay at the seminary and be taught. I often found myself in tears as I witnessed their sincerity and faithfulness. They had an assignment, and they knew it had to be fulfilled. Before I left to come back to the States I asked these pastors to pray over me. As they prayed, the Holy Spirit spoke in perfect English and said, "I am raising you up to become a great leader." May I add, when a 'word' is given such as this, its recipient may never realize when it is fulfilled, because God desires to receive all the glory. Therefore, I raised my head up to see who spoke those words. Only one of the pastors knew a little English, and it wasn't him who spoke.

As I think back and reflect, those pastor's brought encouragement and rekindled a new passion in me. They were committed and willing to learn and knew the task ahead of them was great. They were eager to do whatever it took to fulfill Gods plan.

Are you following the assignment God

instilled within you? Someone that follows their assignment is whole and full of life. They cannot be stopped by circumstances or by people who are miserable because of choosing to follow secondary things.

> *(A)s His divine power has given to us all things that pertain to life and godliness, through the knowledge of Him who called us by glory and virtue,* (II Peter 1:3)

Think about that, God has given us **all things** pertaining to life and godliness.

His assignment will bring peace and wholeness in your life, but more than anything, following His ways will bring satisfaction. Therefore, if you die before He comes back, wouldn't it be great to have as your epitaph, "He (or She) followed their God-given assignment." Remember, a person walks in life and godliness, through the knowledge of God's word. Jesus already paved the way. Christ has all wisdom, so why try to improve on something that's perfect? Seek Christ!

It's a good time to understand that you are

of the seed of Abraham. God told Abram, "Get out," but once he came out he followed God's assignment.

> *And the Scripture was fulfilled which says, "Abraham believed God, and it was accounted to him for righteousness." And he was called the friend of God.* (James 2:23)

Listen to these promises that God gives Abraham.

- ❖ I will show you the land.
- ❖ I will make you a great nation.
- ❖ I will bless you.
- ❖ I will make your name great.
- ❖ You will be a blessing.
- ❖ I will bless them that bless you.
- ❖ I will curse them that curse you.
- ❖ In you all nations (families) will be blessed.

How can anyone have a low self-esteem if he or she follows God's leadership?

There are people all around you right now who fall into three categories. Some people make things happen, some people watch things happen, and other people wonder what happened. If you will decide today to follow God's assignment, you will be the one that makes things happen!

If you follow God's assignment, He will equip and anoint you. Therefore, you will touch others. Right after Jenny and I were married, I landed my first job. It was selling accident Insurance policies. I had to leave my young bride, and stay in a lonely hotel for one week. I was a new believer in the Lord. Fortunately for me, I roomed with a man who had a deep walk with God. When He prayed it seemed as though heaven opened. As I walked with him from the hotel to the training center we would talk. Men and women would gather around him as they heard his testimony. They were drawn because of Gods spirit and he would lead them to salvation. What was happening? This man's anointing had become corporate; it was for anyone and everyone.

God hungers to flow through you into other

people. Whatever you think about our new President, he ran his whole campaign on the saying, "Yes we can!" That's a faith statement if I have ever heard one. If you will believe in yourself as much as God believes in you, many will be influenced for the glory of God. When the early church left the upper room, their assignment was to touch Jerusalem, and then other cities, and then the world. Did they follow it? Oh yes, and you can too by receiving vision and purpose where you are right now.

Abraham decided to follow God, and trust Him because he believed. Yes, Abraham heard from God, but he still had to walk it out daily, and believe for the promise to come to pass. I've heard people say, "I'm not doing it unless God speaks to me." I want to reply, "He already has, through His word."

Abraham believed God, and it was counted unto him for righteousness.　(Romans 4:3)

Abraham was a man of faith.

*Now faith is the substance of things hoped for,
the evidence of things not seen.*

(Hebrews 11:1)

*The fundamental fact of existence is that this
trust in God, this faith, is the firm foundation
under everything that makes life worth living.
It's our handle on what we can't see.*

(Hebrews 11:1 TM)

Real faith is believing now, no matter what.
How could the writer of Hebrews receive such a
powerful revelation about faith? Because he
looked back through time, and saw men and
women of old. There he found a trend. That
trend lead him to rejoice over righteousness.
Enoch, Moses, Abraham, Rahab, Joseph, and
Esther just to name a few. However, the writer
quickly understood that right living could only
be obtained through steadfast devotion unto
God. Faith has to be the ability to leave
unfinished work in the hands of God!

A.W. Tozer once said, "God, being who He
is, cannot cease to be what He is, and being
what He is, He cannot act out of character with

Himself. He is at once faithful and unchanging, so all His words and acts must be and must remain faithful."[3]

If you are living by faith, you have a firm foundation. You have a handle on what you can't see. Let's look at Abraham's assignment, so you can better understand your assignment.

> *(as it is written, "I have made you a father of many nations") in the presence of Him whom he believed—God, who gives life to the dead and calls those things which do not exist as though they did; who, contrary to hope, in hope believed, so that he became the father of many nations, according to what was spoken, "So shall your descendants be. And not being weak in faith, he did not consider his own body, already dead (since he was about a hundred years old), and the deadness of Sarah's womb. He did not waver at the promise of God through unbelief, but was strengthened in faith, giving glory to God, and being fully convinced that what He had promised He was also able to perform. And therefore "it was accounted to him for righteousness." Now it was not written for his sake alone that it was imputed to him, but also for us. It shall be imputed to us who*

*believe in Him who raised up Jesus our Lord
from the dead, who was delivered up because
of our offenses, and was raised because of
our justification.* (Romans 4: 17-25)

As you trust, believe, and walk with God; God will quicken the dead. He gives life back to dead situations. Also, He calls those things which do not exist as though they do. Why? All because you are following your assignment. Sometimes on this road it might seem as if life is an act. You just stay faithful, and God will see you through.

*The strong spirit of a man will sustain him in
bodily pain or trouble.* (Proverbs 18:14 Amp)

You will need to be strong, and filled with courage because it isn't the large mountains that bring a man's spirit down. No, it's the mundane things of life, the daily grind of just showing up with your assignment deep down inside. Remember, Proverbs says, "your strong spirit will sustain you."

The assignment you follow will influence others. Many will catch ablaze because of your faithfulness to follow. Again, sometimes you will not have knowledge of anything changing in your surroundings, but God's assignment working through you will touch and change others. That's because some people plant seeds, while others water them, yet still some individuals will be there for the harvest. I've known people who spent years trying to lead one friend to Christ. Then suddenly, a complete stranger brings that person to salvation. What happened? The seed that had been watered, and taken care of finally sprouted. The harvest will come regardless.

Do not for one-second entertain the thought that your assignment is too small. If you stay faithful to that assignment before you know it, it will bloom and produce.

Do not be deceived, God is not mocked; for whatever a man sows, that he will also reap.
(Galatians 6:7)

The first church I pastored was twelve miles out in the middle of nowhere. I wanted to take a friend of mine, who was also a minister, to see where my church was located. As we traveled down the winding country roads, he began to tell me about his first church. How he could look back, and appreciate the small beginnings. My point is, stop the complaining: one day you too will be able to appreciate where you came from, and how the Lord brought you through. Stop wishing the present away.

I'm sure most of you have seen the movie, "It's a Wonderful Life." George Bailey's world begins to crumble around him, so in a moment of desperation he makes the statement, "I wish I had never been born!" George's angel allowed his wish to come true, and he gets to see what the world would be like without him. He watches the impact that he had on hundreds of people, and on his small town where he lived. Remember, if you will follow the assignment God has for you, you too will impact people, places, and situations.

Then the LORD answered me and said: Write the vision and make it plain on tablets, that he may run who reads it. For the vision is yet for an appointed time; But at the end it will speak, and it will not lie. Though it tarries, wait for it; because it will surely come, It will not tarry. Behold the proud, His soul is not upright in him; but the just shall live by his faith. (Habakkuk 2: 2-4)

Write down your goals. Stop sitting back and waiting. No more hiding. Many people attend a mega-church, so they can hide, and not be accountable to anyone. They can slip in, and out of the service, and no one knows if they were there or not. It takes courage to get out of the pew and get busy. I had a man tell me he had struggled with the fact that his gifting didn't seem to help the church. He decided he wasn't needed in the body. I told him if he was faithful within his occupation, and displayed Christ through his actions, his fruit would bless the body of Christ. He was so relieved. He told me he was going back to church. The burden was lifted. This man is now a light in the midst of darkness on his job. What a blessing! I am telling you right now, "The sky is the limit." God created you for greatness and He has called you to conquer, so begin where you are.

Being confident of this very thing, that He who has begun a good work in you will complete it until the day of Jesus Christ;
(Philippians 1:6)

Stop claiming to be "the seed of Abraham," if you are not walking and talking like he did. Remember, how Jesus rebuked the Jews for proclaiming Abraham as their father when they did not live by faith? Twenty-Five years after God spoke this promise to Abraham, the promise seemed to elude him; however, his soul was filled with confidence that God's words would be fulfilled. Abraham kept himself bound to what God promised him.

He staggered not at the promise of God through unbelief; but was strong in faith giving glory to God.   (Romans 4:20)

Maybe he reminded himself daily by writing it in the dirt, or on rocks. Maybe he rehearsed God's words in his mind, and visualized them

out. However he did it, Abraham decided that
he was not going to be double minded. Someone
who tries to live like that could be classified as a
person with two minds.

> *If any of you lacks wisdom, let him ask of
> God, who gives to all liberally and without
> reproach, and it will be given to him. But let
> him ask in faith, with no doubting, for he who
> doubts is like a wave of the sea driven and
> tossed by the wind. For let not that man
> suppose that he will receive anything from the
> Lord; he is a double-minded man, unstable in
> all his ways.* (James 1:5-8)

The Father is Kingdom-focused, and your
assignment will be Kingdom-focused. You
might say, "But I'm a sales person, how can I
have a Kingdom-focused assignment?"
Whatever direction your job takes you, God's
assignment can be found. Remember this, as a
believer, the fruit of the Spirit, along with His
gifts and callings, will always be inside you.
There will be opportunities for you to influence
a co-worker, friend or stranger. Hence, His
assignment can be carried out. Jesus told us to

pray in Matthew 6, *Thy Kingdom come, thy will be done on earth as it is in heaven.*

> *But seek first the kingdom of God and His righteousness, and all these things shall be added to you."* (Matthew 6:33)

Living in a culture of Western world thinking has deceived many. When you meet a person for the first time, and find out they are a Christian what is the next question you ask them? "Where do you attend church?" One to three hours a week at church does not sum up our walk with the Lord. If you aren't careful, you can have a **churchgoing mentality instead of a *discipleship mentality*!** When you go to church, do you bring a notebook just as a student would?

Are you passionate to hear from God? I remind you, your assignment was given to you because Jesus, God's son, gave His life. My assignments will undoubtedly cost me because whatever I really believe in, I will be willing to invest money, time, and prayer in.

Your assignment will generate faith. Your faith in God will be multiplied and it will touch others. The assignment will produce in me patience, and patience, character and character, hope. (Read Romans 5:1-4) How many of you are ready to both talk and walk the assignment God has for you?

Questions

Can be answered in a group, or as an individual

Have you experienced God's call? In what way?

How does faith direct you?

Do you consider yourself successful?

What brings success?

What is the world's view of success versus the believer's view?

What's your assignment?

What's the body's assignment?

Will you go where God directs you?

How can you be sure it's God directing you?

*Goal Setting: Write down your goals for the next year, month and week.
(It becomes harder as you go because long-range forecasting is exciting, but next week is mundane!)*

Real goals require real work!

Relationships Make or Break

Love never gives up, never loses faith, is always hopeful, and endures through every circumstance."

(I Corinthians 13: 7 NLT)

The Amplified Bible says it this way:

Love bears up under anything and everything that comes, is ever ready to believe the best of every person, its hopes are fadeless under all circumstances, and it endures everything [without weakening].

Relationships require constant attention. They are never maintenance-free. Relationships are like flowers: if you do not nurture and protect them they die. **Every good and lasting relationship is based on love.** In-fact, if love isn't the number one factor that relationship will fail. Think about this: our relationship with God is a good model for our relationship with mankind. God isn't on-and off-again; He is not fickle. No, His love for all humankind is everlasting.

By this we know love, because He laid down His life for us. And we also ought to lay down our lives for the brethren.　(I John 3:16)

May I add, the best place to make and keep relationships is in church. If you can't make associations inside church something is wrong. Think about this: if you forget to feed your dog for two days he's going to be very hungry. However, if you fail to remember him for two weeks he's going to die of starvation. Lasting connections are worth an investment. The deposit you make will allow many withdrawals. You cannot withdraw what you haven't deposited. The relationships you keep are like the seeds that you sow. You will see a harvest. God always blesses a pure heart.

Relationships require feeding; without the proper diet the relationship will dry up. Studies prove that individuals who lack relationships are usually unhealthy. Any relationship has to be mixed with a lot of listening and little talking. Once you learn to listen you will earn the right to talk. Phone calls, letters and e-mails are necessary to grow closer. Many times you call even though you feel they should reach out to you. Why? Because you are working on a friendship that is worth the sacrifice. Jesus said:

> *I am the vine, you are the branches. He who abides in Me, and I in him, bears much fruit; for without Me you can do nothing.*
> (John 15:5)

Doesn't it stand to reason, if you are such a vital part of Christ, that you should know Him? How He speaks, His habits, and His ways? In this one verse Jesus refers to Himself as the vine. In plant life the vine carries all the important life sources so the branches can flourish. However, the vine in itself cannot produce, but when the vine has many branches, both become a force to be reckoned with. Jesus said, you would bear much fruit. The sad part for many individuals is when they try to live without associations. Remember Jesus said,

"Without Me you can do nothing that will last."

Jesus shows how much He is willing to invest in you when He stayed on the cross.

> *He made Him who knew no sin to be sin for us, that we might become the righteousness of God in Him.* (II Corinthians 5:21)

Jesus Christ became sin for you. Now that's a relationship. He could have called legions of angels down but he didn't.

Christ knew no sin. He was made Sin; not a sinner, but Sin, a Sin-offering, a Sacrifice for sin. The end and design of all this was, that we might be made the righteousness of God in him, might be justified freely by the grace of God through the redemption which is in Christ Jesus.(4)

> *A man who has friends must himself be friendly, but there is a friend who sticks closer than a brother.* (Proverbs 18:24)

When you die your money won't give you comfort. The warmth that you will need only comes through relationships. Many people fight against relationships, but these relationships will bring contacts that will help you get where you need to go. Many call this networking.

Networking can be defined as a practice of gathering of contacts. When you learn to network you are not alone. If your job plays out the contacts you have will help you land your next job. This next job might have better benefits and pay. By-no-means should you plan this route if your motives are wrong. In other words, if you plan to network just to get ahead with no regard to the feelings of others, people will see right through you. Your plans will fail!

Unfortunately, I know some people like that. Some seem to live life only to manipulate, and they never grow out of this. If you will base your life on facilitating others, when you need help, your aid will be there. We should all learn from Christ Jesus.

Let this mind be in you which was also in Christ Jesus, who, being in the form of God, did not consider it robbery to be equal with God, but made Himself of no reputation,

*taking the form of a bondservant, and coming
in the likeness of men. And being found in
appearance as a man, He humbled Himself
and became obedient to the point of death,
even the death of the cross. Therefore God
also has highly exalted Him and given Him
the name   which is above every name, that at
the name of Jesus every knee should bow, of
those in heaven, and of those on earth, and of
those under the earth, and that every tongue
should confess that Jesus Christ is Lord, to
the glory of God the Father.*
(Philippians 2:5-8)

Think about verse eight again. Jesus became
obedient to the tree His Father created. Are you
better than Jesus? As a person becomes
obedient to the Lord, God will do the exalting.

Regardless of what kind of relationships you
have, they all need to be birthed from love
because "love never fails." For example: if a
person is selling a product doesn't it stand to
reason that he would mention the name of the
one who gave the referral. Now who would you
buy from, someone whom you are acquainted
with or a stranger? Without others helping you

the dream God placed within you cannot become a reality. We need each other. Many people do not like these ideas because it sounds like politics. Whether you like it or not, whether you call it politics, relationships, or networking it all involves others. Life is all about friendships.

Besides my family, I have a best friend. We have been friends for twenty years. We both have worked hard to keep it. There have been times when we could have stopped caring. However, we have decided to fight for our friendship. Many times when I'm down he'll call. We invest time and forethought in this relationship. I can tell him anything, and he feels the same way.

Someone once said, **"fellowship is like two fellows in a ship: one can't sink the other without sinking himself."** (Think about that.)

Who do you know? Write down a list of people you haven't reached out to lately and contact them. Stop procrastinating. After all, you have the gift of God that someone might need. I have a millionaire friend who stopped at a phone booth several years ago. He was very depressed because one of his businesses were failing. As he opened the phone book a tract fell out. He opened it, and began to read about God's love. All because a stranger left that one tract, this man was born again! You can begin today by praying for people you do not know. Moreover, you might gain a new relationship.

Before you meet your potential client, boss, friend, or date try to find out a few interesting things about them if you can. Perhaps their birthday, or where they were raised. Maybe their hobbies, or their favorite foods. More than likely you will get the job, make the sale, or impress the date. You will make an impression on them greater than someone who comes in, not knowing a single thing about them. Now really, who would you choose?

Sometimes growing involves venturing out of your circle of friends, and family, and making a larger circle of influence. Let me warn you, it could involve pain and rejection from other parties because they won't understand why you are including more people in your life. If this happens, try not to react but strive to walk in love.

> *As a pastor, it amazes me how individuals walk away from relationships, and burn the bridge behind them. Many people don't think anything about burning a relationship bridge. I think multitudes in the body of Christ are holding onto pain, rejection, and even offenses that hold them back from knowing or having God's best. God is all about reconciliation, or mending of broken relationships.*

> *If someone says, "I love God," and hates his brother, he is a liar; for he who does not love his brother whom he has seen, how can he love God whom he has not seen? And this commandment we have from Him: that he who loves God must love his brother also.* (I John 4:20-21)

Most Christians are guilty of the sin of omission. What I mean is, the failure to do something one can and ought to do. If you know you should be friendly, but you hold your feelings back, that's the sin of omission. Just ask the Lord to forgive you, and stop holding back. Listen to some of these excuses: I don't have the time. I don't like them. I heard things about them. I think they should come over and talk to me, or I think the pastor should reach out to them.

Just this week, I had someone tell me they were tired of being hurt by people. Life is all about relationships. Someone who fails in relationships over and over again is usually an individual who hasn't learned their importance or has not learned how to walk in God's love. Ask any CEO why most individuals get fired from their job. They will tell you it is because they do not know how to get along with others. How sad! Believe it or not, prayer can change bad social skills. Ask God to change your heart. Place a high demand upon His word, and before you know it, He will change your very nature.

Here are some truths about relationships:

+ They are never flawless.

✦ Even though two people are born-again, relationships are strained at times.

✦ Relationships require work.

✦ Sometimes relationships are one-sided.

✦ Relationships cannot be put on cruise control.

✦ Relationships take time, a listening ear, phone calls, visits and even money.

✦ There has never been a perfect relationship.

Love must be sincere. Hate what is evil; cling to what is good. Be devoted to one another in brotherly love. Honor one another above yourselves. Never be lacking in zeal, but keep your spiritual fervor, serving the Lord. Be joyful in hope, patient in affliction, faithful in prayer. Share with God's people who are in need. Practice hospitality. Bless those who persecute you; bless and do not curse. Rejoice with those who rejoice; mourn with those who mourn. Live in harmony with one another. Do not be proud, but be willing to associate with people of low position. Do not be conceited. Do not repay anyone evil for evil. Be careful to do what is right in the eyes of everybody. If it is possible, as far as it depends on you, live at peace with everyone. Do not take revenge, my friends, but leave room for God's wrath, for it is written: "It is mine to avenge; I will repay," says the Lord. On the contrary:" If your enemy is hungry, feed him; if he is thirsty, give him something to drink. In doing this, you will heap burning coals on his head." Do not be overcome by evil, but overcome evil with good. (Romans 12:9-21)

Again I say, "If your motive is wrong God sees right into the inner man."

Let's break this down,

✦ Love one another; Cling to love, and hate evil.

✦ Honor each other. Value listening, other's will be drawn to you.

✦ Worship with others, invite zeal and passion to come <u>around</u> and <u>within</u>.

✦ Give to one another. (No selfish hermits allowed.)

✦ Bless those who hate you. Just remember, **they must not know you, because if they knew you, they would love you**.

✦ Show compassion to one another. Become sensitive.

✦ Live in humility with each other. Don't be a know it all.

✦ Invite peace daily. Peace must not become a forgotten element.

✦ Don't defend yourself-Bite the bullet. In other words, be willing to take the blame even when it's not your fault. (However, Stand up for yourself when needed.)

✦ Keep every relationship in the Lord's hands.

Notice, it's all about others; giving your best to others. As you live in this manner, you show the mark of true maturity. Knowing who you are in Christ is essential.

Here's a prime example in Luke 19:1-10. Jesus was passing by Jericho when He noticed a man named Zacchaeus in a tree. Was this man righteous? Far from it. He was known as a user. Today, he would be thrown in prison for scamming people. Jesus stopped and spoke to his need. Zacchaeus' need was basic: he needed a friend. So Jesus invited Himself to his house that day, and ate with him. Then Jesus led Zacchaeus into salvation. Why? Because Jesus was willing to invest His life, and time into this man whom everyone else had given up on. One man in a tree was important to Jesus.

Will you commit with me to gain new associations? Your dealings with people are important to Christ. He will love them through you if you ask for His help. Remember this, what you do, and think today will affect tomorrow. "What you make happen for others, God will make happen for you." Your relationships will follow you all through life.

Questions

Can be answered in a group, or as an individual

Do you have some relationships that need mending? *(Read John 15)*

List some names of friends you could call.

How do you define relationships?

List several ways you can work on them.

Are you a good listener?

Do you burn bridges? If so, how many? How can you repair them?

Do you network?

How can you do a better job?

Can you talk to a complete stranger better than
someone who knows you?

Will you commit with me to gain new
associations?

Do you keep your word?

Can friends trust you?

I Do

After the man and woman say those famous words "I Do" the fun begins. The honeymoon has been greatly anticipated and so off they go. Life is amazing as the two become one.

As I dated Jenny I kept secrets from her about my past. I thought she would not like me if she knew the real person I was. What lies we can feed ourselves! Be honest and try to reveal what is in your dark closets before you say "I do." That way there won't be too much of a shock when the honeymoon is over. Going back to my marriage, after the honeymoon the "real me" began to manifest. I'm sure Jenny thought, "What have I gotten myself into?"

Realizing we needed to make a truce, both of us pledged never to mention the **"D word"** (divorce). We also adopted a seventy times seven policy. And boy, we used it... a lot. This policy was based on the scripture where Jesus told Peter when asked, "how many times a day should we forgive," Jesus answered, "Seventy times seven." The first year of marriage was tough because there were so many adjustments. It usually is a difficult time. The secret in that first year of marriage is communication, and openness to change because you now have a partner for life.

I cannot imagine marrying an unbeliever, or someone with another kind of faith in a false god. Especially if that person refuses to convert before the marriage takes place. Thankfully, Jenny and I had prayer in common. One of Jenny's questions to me as we were dating was, "Howard, if the devil were to come in our house could you get him out?"

I said, **"I'll run him off!"**

Be sober, be vigilant; because your adversary the devil walks about like a roaring lion, seeking whom he may devour. Resist him, steadfast in the faith, knowing that the same sufferings are experienced by your brotherhood in the world." (I Peter 5:8-9)

When we hit a wall of anger and distrust we

knew that we had to go to God with our pain. Sometimes young men, and women feel desperate and they end up marrying outside of their faith. As a true believer in Christ you must wait for the right person who desires to walk hand in hand with you. Listen to me, he or she will not change after marriage. You will most likely have to serve their god. Please wait on God's selection for you and not your own.

Most marriages that end up in divorce are because of three things that should be addressed before you say, "I do." These three subjects are pride, money and religion. All of these should be considered with care. Do not take it for granted that they will just somehow work themselves out.

Before I address these, let me add, many adults think living together for a while is the answer. While living together may seem to make sense, it really isn't the measuring stick it is presumed to be. The couple is excited and they are simply enthralled with each other. As the relationship grows, and they feel they are compatible they begin to dream of getting married. There is this romantic notion involving the anticipated nuptials that keep a couple's fairy-tale dream alive. The bride-to-be may be fantasizing about the wedding no matter how big or small, while the husband to be is just basking in her apparent joy. But when the marriage is sealed before God and witnesses, and the honeymoon is over, everything changes. Now they face the daily grind of work, paying bills and sometimes seeing the worst in their spouse.

What they thought was so wonderful now appears to be a terrible mistake. This is primarily because Satan hates union and covenant. He was thrown out of heaven because of pride, and his unwillingness to submit. These verses accurately describe the fallen one. The devil.

How you are fallen from heaven, O shining star, son of the morning! You have been thrown down to the earth, you who destroyed the nations of the world. For you said to

yourself, 'I will ascend to heaven and set my throne above God's stars. I will preside on the mountain of the gods far away in the north. I will climb to the highest heavens and be like the Most High.' Instead, you will be brought down to the place of the dead, down to its lowest depths. Everyone there will stare at you and ask, 'Can this be the one who shook the earth and made the kingdoms of the world tremble? Is this the one who destroyed the world and made it into a wasteland? Is this the king who demolished the world's greatest cities and had no mercy on his prisoners?
(Isaiah 14:12-17)

God Himself ordained marriage, where two shall become one flesh. This brings me back to the pride issue mentioned earlier. The devil understands that there is power and unity when two become one. He conjures up schemes in each other's thoughts to keep pride in.

The weapons we fight with are not the weapons of the world. On the contrary, they have divine power to demolish strongholds. We demolish arguments and every pretension that sets itself up against the knowledge of

God, and we take captive every thought to
make it obedient to Christ."

(II Corinthians 10:4-5 NIV)

Learning to forgive quickly is a key
ingredient. One of my worst problems came
because of unresolved anger. I learned how to
cry out to God not with fancy words, but with a
heart that was desperate for change. I would
cry, "Lord, fill me with love, take all anger and
pride out. Please Lord, fill me with love." This
brought a wonderful meltdown of myself.

I identified myself completely with him.
Indeed, I have been crucified with Christ. My
ego is no longer central. It is no longer
important that I appear righteous before you
or have your good opinion, and I am no
longer driven to impress God. Christ lives in
me. The life you see me living is not "mine,"
but it is lived by faith in the Son of God, who
loved me and gave himself for me. I am not
going to go back on that.

(Galatians 2:20 TM)

The second issue is money. It's rarely
thought about while dating, but after the

honeymoon reality hits. That which is his becomes hers and vice versa. Suddenly, both parties look at money and the checkbook, and couples become paranoid about each other. Before marriage, each spent their money on themselves, but now the payroll checks must be shared. The first ten percent belongs to God. Then ten percent should be saved. Finally eighty percent is used to pay bills.

It is estimated that in 2009, more people will file bankruptcy than will graduate from college. The number one cause of divorce in North America today is conflict over money and its management.

If possible have a date night, tuck back some money, and become creative. It does not take a lot of money to have fun. **Pack a lunch; go on a hike or a picnic together.** You will find that it's the simple things in life that make memories. My advice is, decide who will handle the checkbook and always be open. Before making large purchases talk about them. Of course, a sizable order for some might be their grocery selections. For others, it could be a new television. Go together, shop together, and talk. Before making a large find list the pros and cons of the selection. Ask yourselves, "Do we really need this?"

Growing up, my parents owned a retail store. On a Saturday night the store caught on fire. It was near Christmas, so they had extra inventory upstairs. I was just a little boy, but I can remember seeing the smoke from our house about four miles away. My parents were under-insured, so they lost around 300,000 dollars in merchandise in just a few hours. That was a lot of money back in the 70's.

I can remember like it was yesterday. The next morning, with only a little money in their checking account, my mother asked my dad, **"Are we going to tithe today?"**

My dad looked at mom and said, "We have to tithe and keep the Lord first." When my parents rebuilt, their store did better than ever! That was 39 years ago, but what an impression this had on me! (Not the fire, but my parent's reaction and their love for God.) I am blessed.

Credit cards should be limited to just one, and no more than two. Maybe one of you comes into this new union never lacking because of your upbringing. The other comes from a family that is very frugal. My advice would be for the one who never did without to conform to the spendthrift. More than likely, the person who comes from the family who never did without, also had a family with much stress or who owed big debt. You have heard the saying, "Ask a millionaire how much is enough and they will say, "just a little bit more." Debt and stress are killers both physically and spiritually. Money is not the root of all evil. No, it's the love of money.

If you will put God first in your marriage it will work. Men are totally geared differently than women. Men are moved by looks. Women are wired to need more emotional support.

When this support is lacking the lady can feel as though she's been abandoned. If the male is insensitive to her needs, she won't connect with him. A man may think, "If she just sees my big muscles she will be impressed." He fails to listen to her. Remember this, she doesn't see the skin without hearing the heart. The lady cries out, "Date me, send me flowers, or write me a love letter."

The male is thinking, "She will like my shiny car." However, she doesn't seem to care.

Why? Maybe because God created man in His own image, while the woman came from the man. The female needs emotional support from the male to feel significant because she came from his flesh. A man is never satisfied until he is fully surrendered unto Christ. A man without Christ is a man who usually flounders from one thing to another.

Each man has been called to be the priest of his home. When the male drinks, or has other destructive habits, and he pays no attention to his family, his family will suffer. Men, God has called you to bless your family with the words you speak. What comes from you mouth?

*And the LORD spoke to Moses, saying:
"Speak to Aaron and his sons, saying, 'This is
the way you shall bless the children of Israel.
Say to them: "The LORD bless you and keep
you; The LORD make His face shine upon
you, And be gracious to you; The LORD lift
up His countenance upon you, And give you
peace." "So they shall put My name on the
children of Israel, and I will bless them."*
(Numbers 6:22-27)

Many Jewish people speak this blessing over
their children daily. This blessing can be spoken
over your wife or even your job. This is a
blessing I speak over my youngest child every
morning as I take him to school. Remember,
God blesses you, and He has called you to bless
your family.

Often the woman has to play the role of both
mother and priest. This isn't normal, nor is it
God's plan. Sadly, many women are forced to do
this, and the Lord certainly blesses their efforts.
I believe that the male, the priest, will be held
very accountable on Judgment Day.

God will ask hard questions like, "Why
didn't you take your family to My church and

worship Me? Why didn't you spend quality time with your family?"

You might say, "Well, God I've been busy making money, or I wanted to do my own thing." The Twenty-First Century Church is in jeopardy primarily because the generations before them had little to no commitment to the Sabbath. As a young lad I remember the "Blue Laws." Now you know my age. Going back, when one generation fails the next one suffers. I say to you, stop making excuses and get committed. Your children need it, and they deserve God's best.

> *Those who are planted in the house of the LORD shall flourish in the courts of our God. They shall still bear fruit in old age; They shall be fresh and flourishing.*
> (Psalm 92:13-14)

> *Husbands, love your wives, just as Christ also loved the church and gave Himself for her."*
> (Ephesian 5:25)

That is a tall order, but men, this is what you were created to do. You are to be that type of covering for your wife. When you do this, you will find that you will have a new woman. Every lady desires to have this from their man unless they were raised in some sort of dysfunctional environment. Think about that verse again, Christ loved His church so much He gave Himself up for her. In spite of its many flaws and failures, Jesus Christ loves His church. Men, regardless of what you think about your wife, love her as Christ loves the church. You will not go wrong. Most men are looking for their wives to be totally submissive to them.

> *Wives, submit to your own husbands, as to the Lord.* (Ephesians 5: 22)

The wife cannot, for safety's sake, stay submissive to a man who doesn't take the spiritual lead in the house. If the man isn't the priest, he will play some sort of lower role. He will be double minded, and unstable. Isn't it sad to think about God's created being choosing second place? I place high emphasis on every husband. I believe that the Bible backs up this statement "As the man goes, so will his whole family."

Any male can party and do his own thing, but it takes a true man (a man of God) to put the Lord God first and be the spiritual leader of his house. As the husband takes his rightful role, the wife might not believe it's true at first, but continue to be faithful. You will be the richest man in the world.

It's sad to see so many boys and girls grow up not having their proper identity. Husbands who won't make a covenant with God become men who pass their poor spiritual genes onto their children. A wife sometimes looks for affection outside the confines of her home because she is married to a little boy with a man's body. She's tired of changing his diapers! Husbands, you have the ability to set your wife free. When a boy does not have a man figure in their lives, how sad it is. No wonder we have a gender identity problem.

What's more sad to me is these boys grow up not knowing how to treat their wife, and the cycle goes on. To break this terrible pattern in ones life, it will take new dedication to the Creator. When this dedication doesn't happen, or is carried out halfheartedly, the spouse knows, and the children begin to realize something is missing. The children will grow up with resentment. They make a commitment in their heart not to be like their father. This cycle is hard to break. Some families expect their local church or youth pastor to make all the difference in their children. However, everything begins, and ends at home. Men, we need spiritual fathers, leaders, and priests.

Fathers, spend time with your children. If they are young make a commitment to read one chapter from the Bible each night to them. You will be blessed, and they will too! Your wife will naturally see this new commitment. She will be touched because her children are part of her. Your commitment and discipline to devotion time will ingrain new-life-goals and love inside your little ones.

The rain and snow come down from the heavens and stay on the ground to water the earth. They cause the grain to grow; producing seed for the farmer and bread for the hungry. it is the same with my word. I send it out, and it always produces fruit. It will accomplish all I want it to, and it will prosper everywhere I send it."
(Isaiah 55:10-11 NLT)

Sometimes parents think they need to be their children's best friend. Children need their parents to become spiritual role models, and disciplined spiritual leaders more than they need a buddy. Children will always allow you to speak truth to them, if they see you leading the way.

I have noticed many times our roles seem to be turned around with the child portraying the parent. What's going on? Usually there is failure within the parent, so the parent thinks that if he or she can just be like, or act similar to the child the youngster will approve. No. Children need Godly parents.

Train up a child in the way he should go, And when he is old he will not depart from it."
(Proverbs 22: 6)

Another issue in life is the art of being content whether you are single, a single parent, or married with children. In life you see many seasons. Singles long to be married. They fail to appreciate their ability to use this time to concentrate only on God, and perhaps on building their career. All they can see is that they feel lonely for companionship. They don't recognize they are to be one with the Lord. During this time, God will give them the desire of their heart—if they will worship while waiting. This is called contentment, my friend.

Then there are young couples that can't wait for the day they say, "I Do!" They work for a bigger house and long to hear the pitter-pat of little feet. The children come along and life takes more out of them than they knew it could. The demands of child rearing can be overwhelming. So, they start longing for the child to grow up, and leave home. They think joy comes through quietness. Later, as they are older and alone, the couple begins to dream of having grandchildren. They can't wait to buy clothes, and toys for their new grand-baby.

There's an old song called "Anticipation." If you think about it, there is a real message in this song. You keep on longing for something more instead of recognizing that these are the good old days. The cycle goes on, the seasons come and go. Each one can be a stepping stone to a better you.

Enjoy your life now. This is called contentment. Remember, joy and peace are only found through Jesus Christ. Jesus is the only one who can give you true happiness.

Think back on those early days when you first learned about Christ. Remember how you remained faithful even though it meant terrible suffering. (Hebrews 10: 32 NLT)

Questions

Can be answered in a group, or as an individual

Before you say, "I do" will you seek counsel?

How important is it for you to marry a believer?

Will you change your faith for your fiancé?

How committed will you be to your local church?

What do you enjoy together?

Who will handle the bills?

What would change your mind, or make you think twice about marriage?

What's your vision for the two of you?

How often will you visit family?

Do you desire to further your education?

How can you find contentment?

Rejecting Negativism

Finally, brethren, whatever things are true, whatever things are noble, whatever things are just, whatever things are pure, whatever things are lovely, whatever things are of good report, if there is any virtue and if there is anything praiseworthy—meditate on these things. (Philippians 4:8)

Be aware that Paul wrote this letter while he was in prison. A person should come to the conclusion that becoming negative does not have anything to do with physical condition, or the atmosphere. Becoming negative occurs when you take your eyes off the Son of God.

When ones mind is far from God negativism becomes the norm. The works of the flesh push men on to another mundane day. Nothing to look forward to.

My parents love to camp. Not long ago, as my parents were camping, early one morning, my dad went outside. He finds his neighbor standing next to his camper, and goes over to meet him and strikes up a conversation. Dad notices that the man can hardly walk and is in bad shape. As dad talks, he mentions the Lord, and how God has brought him through many spiritual storms. The man's response was an empty expression and an angry rebuttal. He said, "I don't believe in any of that mess!" What a sad scenario, an individual facing death's door, without hope of eternity. There are people around you right now who are living with the same mess, hopelessness. There's nothing sadder than talking to a family who just lost there son, and have no hope for the future. They were too busy for God, and His church how sad.

Since you have been raised to new life with Christ, set your sights on the realities of heaven, where Christ sits in the place of honor at God's right hand. Think about the things of heaven, not the things of earth.
(Colossians 3:1-2 NLT)

As I ponder on Philippians 4:8, I have to think long and hard to find something so true, noble, just, pure, and lovely. Some things might fit this category, but how long do they stay this wonderful? I felt the nudge of the Holy Spirit say, "Only Jesus Christ stays and remains the same forever."

> *Jesus Christ is the same yesterday, today, and forever.* (Hebrews 13:8)

Pure, lovely, and just. Mere words can never give Christ justice. You should learn from the past, so you will not be prone to repeat those mistakes. As men of old walked in God's obedience they were always challenged. The voice of negativism, opinions of men, and plain out disobedience will speak. Times have changed, but Satan still works the same way. He knows if he can steal the hope you have and get you thinking wrong, he has you.

> *The thief's purpose is to steal and kill and destroy. My purpose is to give them a rich and satisfying life.* (John 10:10 NLT)

> *And the LORD spoke to Moses, saying, "Send men to spy out the land of Canaan, which I*

*am giving to the children of Israel. From each
tribe of their fathers you shall send a man,
every one a leader among them." Then they
told him, and said: "We went to the land
where you sent us. It truly flows with milk and
honey, and this is its fruit. Nevertheless the
people who dwell in the land are strong; the
cities are fortified and very large; moreover
we saw the descendants of Anak there. The
Amalekites dwell in the land of the South; the
Hittites, the Jebusites, and the Amorites dwell
in the mountains; and the Canaanites dwell
by the sea and along the banks of the
Jordan." Then Caleb quieted the people
before Moses, and said, "Let us go up at once
and take possession, for we are well able to
overcome it." But the men who had gone up
with him said, "We are not able to go up
against the people, for they are stronger than
we." And they gave the children of Israel a
bad report of the land which they had spied
out, saying, "The land through which we have
gone as spies is a land that devours its
inhabitants, and all the people whom we saw
in it are men of great stature. There we saw
the giants (the descendants of Anak came
from the giants); and we were like
grasshoppers in our own sight, and so we
were in their sight."*

                              (Numbers 13:1-2, 27-33)

Faith cries out, "You are well able!" Doubt whispers, "You can't do it; you are too small. You're not able; moreover, you're not smart enough. You aren't in their league."

Real faith calculates the cost, however, it never refuses to back down because of fear. I have heard it said that the greatest ideas are buried in the graves of men and women who became afraid of the task set before them. God forbid.

I have an aunt and uncle named Richard and Donna. Every summer they would invite my brother, Harry, and I to stay with them for a week. Of course, they have children close to our age. They lived on a golf course. Every summer, my cousins and I wanted to go to a very popular attraction in Atlanta. So we figured out a way to go practically for nothing.

We would take several days and find hundreds of golf balls. It was so much fun! Then we would wash each ball, and categorize its name and condition. My cousin, and I were the youngest, so we were in charge of selling the balls. In fact, we enjoyed it so much that we would have done it for free. Usually, two or four men would play together. Chris and I would display our abilities of being cute. Before long, another five dollars or so would be added for our trip. There were very few people who turned us down. If they did, we would just wait for the next players. Hint, You won't go wrong if you believe in what you are doing.

Whatever you do in life don't be afraid of failure. If you fail it's just another stepping-stone to learn. **Try your best to learn a trade in life that you would actually do for free**. Then you will have fun and make money. What's wrong with loving what you do?

Chapter 14 says that Israel refused to enter into their promise land. So Joshua and Caleb tore their clothes, and wept. Negativism makes a faith-filled person want to weep. It's tough to fight a pessimistic Spirit. This Spirit can break down the greatest thinkers. It can make them feel paralyzed through and through. The sad part of this story, and many individuals stories, is that God has said He's given them the land.

*Then Caleb quieted the people before Moses,
and said, "Let us go up at once and take
possession, for we are well able to overcome
it."*   (Numbers 13:30)

*You belong to God, my dear children. You
have already won a victory over those people,
because the Spirit who lives in you is greater
than the spirit who lives in the world."*
                    (I John 4:4 NLT)

A bad report can become a faith killer,
especially when those who have a bad report are
just religious and will not change—not even for
God's word. Some people desire what they had
years ago, and no more. How heartbreaking.

Jesus paid the price for everyone to walk
free of negativism and to walk in strong faith. If
you haven't noticed, being negative is in. I said
it, "<u>Being negative is in</u>!" The TV news media
leans totally to negativism because it sells.
Sitcoms are pessimistic, reality shows are
mostly crude, and talk shows are typically
nonconstructive. Most music is negative.
newspapers and magazines are all downbeat. To
break this, it takes a daily dose of Jesus Christ,

and meditating upon His word!

> *"Is not My word like a fire?" says the*
> *LORD, "And like a hammer that breaks the*
> *rock in pieces?"*   (Jeremiah 23:29)

Listen to these verses from the Message
Bible:

> *God means what he says. What he says goes.*
> *His powerful Word is sharp as a surgeon's*
> *scalpel, cutting through everything, whether*
> *doubt or defense, laying us open to listen and*
> *obey. Nothing and no one is impervious to*
> *God's Word. We can't get away from it—no*
> *matter what.*   (Hebrews 4:12-13 TM)

Speak God's word over every situation. "If
you can't speak God's word, should you even
speak?" Again I say there is a Spirit of
negativism upon the land. Can you imagine
getting on a talk show to air your dirty laundry
with titles like "I'm sleeping with my uncle" or
"I'm not the person you think I am?" Women
fighting women, while men threaten to kill their
own brothers. It's hard to believe this stuff sells.
For many people, negative attention is better

than no attention at all. These people will cry out for more, as long as someone will notice them. How hopeless our society has become. Truly we are undone without God. His power is so much greater than what can even imagine.

Jesus said to him, "If you can believe, all things are possible to him who believes."
(Mark 9:23)

Faith in Christ is the only way to destroy the Spirit of doubt.

Negativism doesn't even consider God's promises.

For Jesus Christ, the Son of God, does not waver between "Yes" and "No." He is the one whom Silas, Timothy, and I preached to you, and as God's ultimate "Yes," he always does what he says. For all of God's promises have been fulfilled in Christ with a resounding "Yes!" And through Christ, our "Amen" (which means "Yes") ascends to God for his glory.
(II Corinthians 1:19-20 NLT)

If the devil can keep you negative, you can't

be thankful. Around Thanksgiving you might carve a turkey, and have some dressing, but if you are negative you won't be thankful. As a believer, you should count your blessings daily.

Make a joyful shout to the LORD, all you lands! Serve the LORD with gladness; come before His presence with singing. Know that the LORD, He is God; it is He who has made us, and not we ourselves; we are His people and the sheep of His pasture. Enter into His gates with thanksgiving, And into His courts with praise. Be thankful to Him, and bless His name. For the LORD is good; His mercy is everlasting, And His truth endures to all generations. (Psalm 100:1-5)

Breaking through negativism has to become a lifestyle. Psalm 100 begins by using the word "Make." Sometimes you have to generate praise. Some might say that could be labeled as fake, but I call it faith. The flesh is contrary to the voice of praise. It wants to do it's own thing. When you submit yourself to praise, your Spirit man rises up. We all need Him to arise.

So humble yourselves before God. Resist the devil, and he will flee from you.

(James 4:7)

Suddenly the first verse makes sense to you. You will begin to open your mouth, and make a joyful shout unto to the LORD! I think many times we just need to let go, and open our mouths to Him.

Suppose you were at a football game watching your child play. The quarterback throws the ball to your son with five seconds left on the clock; he goes up for the catch with two opponents guarding him. He catches the ball, and runs for the touch down. Do you think you would just sit there with your mouth shut? I think not. Well, our Lord God desires our praise. After all, He paid the price for all mankind to be saved, healed, and delivered! **I challenge you to try praise, It will change your life.**

Also God's word tells you that you should serve the Lord with gladness. I am so thankful that serving the Lord isn't a grievance, but a pleasure. Why do you serve God with a cold heart? You have been inundated with waves of unbelief, and it's hard to come to the Lord with singing. If you will become excited about God's presence again He will come and burst into your world like never before.

Arise, shine; For your light has come! And the glory of the LORD is risen upon you.
(Isaiah 60:1)

God is not listening to the tone of your voice. He hears your heart and emotions that are vented to Him.

In everything give thanks; for this is the will of God in Christ Jesus for you.
(I Thessalonians 5:18)

It's God's will for you to give thanks not for everything, but in everything. If you have knowledge that the Lord is good, it's probably not enough. However, If you have experienced God's goodness, then you will hunger to stay close to Him. He will sing along with you through life!

It's time for believers to make the effort to be thankful. Some people choose to live life filled with bad memories of the past. They can tell you everything that went wrong. They seem to have memory lapse when it comes to God's goodness. If you are easily pulled into pity parties but you want to change your habitual complaining, there is hope.

> *Through the LORD's mercies we are not consumed, Because His compassions fail not. They are new every morning; Great is Your faithfulness.* (Lamentations 3:22-23)

Enter in His gates with thanksgiving. Before you enter into the Lord's courts, you first have to make up your mind to enter into His gates with the proper attitude. You have to come to the gate and walk through it. Then you can go farther. Many people stop at the gates because they refuse to praise. They just live close to the gates and wonder why things aren't better.

Don't expect to get anywhere with your praise if you have been fighting with your family at home, or doing something underhanded. Ask

Him to forgive your finger pointing, and anger.
Remember, God sees the heart of mankind.

> *For the eyes of the LORD run to and fro*
> *throughout the whole earth, to show Himself*
> *strong on behalf of those whose heart is loyal*
> *to Him. In this you have done foolishly;*
> *therefore from now on you shall have wars."*
> *Then Asa was angry with the seer, and put*
> *him in prison, for he was enraged at him*
> *because of this. And Asa oppressed some of*
> *the people at that time.*
>   (II Chronicles 16: 9-10)

Just as God knew Asa's heart, God knows
your heart. God is good; He is real good. His
word tells us to taste and see that the Lord is
good. God has given all mankind the chance to
know Him through His attributes, and His
creation. (Read the first chapter of Romans.)

> *Send men to spy out the land of Canaan,*
> *which I am giving to the children of Israel...*
>   (Numbers 13:2a)

Some people will be negative no matter
what. Let's say, one hundred people get saved in
the church. These negative people will say,

"Well that's good, but something bad will happen, just wait."

And Jesus answering saith unto them, Have faith in God. For verily I say unto you, That whosoever shall say unto this mountain, Be thou removed, and be thou cast into the sea; and shall not doubt in his heart, but shall believe that those things which he saith shall come to pass; he shall have whatsoever he saith. Therefore I say unto you, What things soever ye desire, when ye pray, believe that ye receive them, and ye shall have them. (Mark 11:22-24 KJ)

You have been entitled to invoke, or summon the very presence of God. You've been called to proclaim His praises. No one can do this better than you. God's angels have not experienced salvation, but you have.

While in the wilderness, over a million Israelites died because of their negativism. I remember reading where someone said that Moses would have to perform a funeral every 30 seconds for 40 years to bury these men and women because of their negative Spirit. No wonder these people were so hopeless. Many Christians say things like, "I'm thankful for my job but...." Or "I'm thankful for my kids but...." Or "I'm thankful for my house but...." **The "but" conjunction is a spiritual malfunction, and can cause real problems. Isn't it sad that unbelief destroys good people?**

As a pastor for twenty years, I have dealt with men and women who were negative. Thinking back on these people, I can honestly say I have never seen anything good come out of faithlessness. It destroys, and does much harm. God has called you to a lifestyle of thanksgiving. Do you have a roof over your head, health, food in your stomach, or most importantly salvation? If you said yes to one of these you can be a thankful person!

*Now these things became our **examples**, to the intent that we should not lust after evil things as they also lusted. And do not become idolaters as were some of them. As it is written, "The people sat down to eat and drink, and rose up to play." Nor let us commit*

*sexual immorality, as some of them did, and in one day twenty-three thousand fell; nor let us tempt Christ, as some of them also tempted, and were destroyed by serpents; **nor complain**, as some of them also complained, and **were destroyed by the destroyer**. Now all these things happened to them as **examples**, and they were written for our admonition, upon whom the ends of the ages have come.*
(I Corinthians 10:6-11)

Paul clearly writes that this is for our example. In other words, Paul inscribes this so you will not go down that same road of complaining and doubting as these Israelites did. Think about this, 10 of the 12 spies were leaders over their tribe, and they were negative. Leaders being negative. The followers didn't have a chance.

First, you know you are in trouble when you study the genealogy of your enemy. Ten of these leaders knew more about their enemy than they did about their God! You know you are in trouble when you see yourself as an insect. Remember this, when you have this negative mentality others will see you as an insect, too.

In I Corinthians 10, God warns us not to become negative, or there will be consequences. Here are seven traits of negativism.

- ✣ They rub off on others.
- ✣ They don't operate in faith.
- ✣ They live below their privileges.
- ✣ They only have negative friends.
- ✣ They never get excited for things of God.
- ✣ They aren't fun.
- ✣ They're lonely.

Be anxious for nothing, but in everything by prayer and supplication, with thanksgiving, let your requests be made known to God; and the peace of God, which surpasses all understanding, will guard your hearts and minds through Christ Jesus.
(Philippians 4:6-7)

Remember how the King James version starts off in verse 6: "Be careful for nothing...." In this twenty-first century can you imagine telling someone you love as they leave, "Be careful for nothing!" That's how you should really live. To be carefree. Think about that.

Being thankful will break the back of the Spirit of negativism. We are a nation that needs the peace of God.

Questions

Can be answered in a group, or as an individual

What thoughts do you think on during the day?

Being honest, what has unbelief stolen from you?

Do you complain a lot?

Can you keep your mouth shut when a negative person talks or do you join in?

Are you the one who starts negative conversations?

In general are you optimistic or pessimistic? (Ask that question of someone who knows you well.)

How can you change?

List 3 things you are thankful for:

Walking In Increase

Oh, sing to the LORD a new song! Sing to the LORD, all the earth. Sing to the LORD, bless His name; proclaim the good news of His salvation from day to day. Declare His glory among the nations, His wonders among all people. (Psalm 96:1-3)

Psalm 96, 98, and 149 all open with the exhortation to sing a new song unto the Lord. Also these Psalms, along with Psalm 105 and 106, are included in David's song of praise. In I Chronicles 16, the Ark of God was positioned in its proper place. From the very beginning the Ark of the Covenant was God's way of positioning man's heart to His glory. The Ark housed God's Presence, and could only be approached by those who had clean hands, and a pure heart. Some have treated the Ark as though it were ordinary, but there is nothing ordinary about God. He is forever present, all-powerful, and all knowing.

This is the song of praise unto God.

Sing to the LORD, all the earth;Proclaim the good news of His salvation from day to day. Declare His glory among the nations, His wonders among all peoples. For the LORD is great and greatly to be praised; He is also to be feared above all gods. For all the gods of the peoples are idols, But the LORD made the heavens. Honor and majesty are before Him; Strength and gladness are in His place. Give to the LORD, O families of the peoples, Give to the LORD glory and strength. Give to the LORD the glory due His name;Bring an offering, and come before Him. Oh, worship the LORD in the beauty of holiness! Tremble before Him, all the earth. The world also is firmly established, It shall not be moved. Let the heavens rejoice, and let the earth be glad; And let them say among the nations, "The LORD reigns. (1 Chronicles 16:23-31)

From the Old Testament to the New, God's ways haven't changed. He is truly worthy to praise and adore.

Regardless of the area where you need increase, God is able! God is the God of abundance. His abundance brings joy.

Like most people, I have many relatives. Joy

is one of my aunts. Her name fits her well. Ray and Joy became successful in their business.

But as a small boy, I can remember back in the day, my Uncle Ray and Aunt Joy starting off in their new venture. Joy would find her way inside a neighbors house and before she knew it, she would book a party. As all the neighbors came over and gathered together, she would tell them her name. She'd make the sales pitch, then stand up on one of the largest bowls she sold and spin around. Everyone loved her personality because the joy of the Lord attracts!

> *The blessing of the Lord makes a person rich, and he adds no sorrow with it.*
> (Proverbs 10:22 NLT)

Abundance of love, joy and peace. The Lord is worth a new song. He gives songs in the dark of night, songs in bitter despair, and songs to the poor. Songs to the depressed, and songs to the weary. Whatever the situation, good or bad God gives songs. God doesn't look at skin color, nor does He think about continents as He blesses. He blesses those who will trust Him. So what really are God's blessings? Without a doubt God's blessings begin with an individual's thoughts and deeds.

I know people who have material possessions but no inward stability or character. True increase always comes when a person learns to give unto God.

> *See those people polishing their chariots, and those others grooming their horses? But we're making garlands for God, our God. The chariots will rust, those horses pull up lame— and we'll be on our feet, standing tall.* (Psalm 20:7-8 TM)

In Genesis, God's word says, "Nothing was created or formed without Him!" God created man in His own likeness, but man was just a mere object until God blew His breath of life within. Think about that: Adam was quickened, or made alive by the Maker Himself. Even though God hasn't blown His physical breath upon you, you are born again. He's made you alive, and quickened you by the Holy Spirit.

*Blessed be the God and Father of our Lord
Jesus Christ, who has blessed us with every
spiritual blessing in the heavenly places in
Christ,*   (Ephesians 1:3)

Now mankind can live, talk, and act with full
redemption because of Jesus Christ becoming
our second Adam.

Think about the word Increase. God never
brings decrease to His children. The times we
think He's forgotten or doesn't care, He's doing
something larger than what the weatherman
can predict. He's bigger than the news alert.
Now do not think for one-second that my
statement is just another prosperity message.
I'm going to give you another point of view on
the importance of increase.

*Oh; sing to the LORD a new song! Sing to the
LORD, all the earth. Sing to the LORD, bless
His name; proclaim the good news of His
salvation from day to day. "*
                         (Psalm 96:1-2)

You need to make this proclamation from
day to day.

*Let them shout for joy and be glad, Who favor
my righteous cause; And let them say
continually, "Let the LORD be magnified,
Who has pleasure in the prosperity of His
servant."* (Psalm 35:27)

First, you are commissioned to shout for joy and be glad. How? By faith. **Secondly**, you are to continually magnify the Lord. Whatever you are facing, begin this new phase. **Finally,** you should know God has pleasure in your prosperity. Now you are set, go for it.

I realize you can't go around singing all day; however, what comes out of your mouth really becomes your song. **You sing what you say.** If you are a negative person the blues will find it's way out of you. It might begin with a cunning remark, or a sour look, but what's inside will be seen, and heard by others.

*A good man out of the good treasure of his
heart brings forth good; and an evil man out
of the evil treasure of his heart brings forth
evil. For out of the abundance of the heart his
mouth speaks.* (Luke 6:45)

How God anointed Jesus of Nazareth with the
Holy Spirit and with power, who went about
doing good and healing all who were
oppressed by the devil, for God was with Him.
(Acts 10:38)

Was Jesus concerned with increase? He sure was. That's why He went about doing good and healing all. He does not want you to live with lack or doubt. If you do go through seasons that are dull and dry, Christ will bring you through richer. He desires for you to live with joy, and peace knowing that lack will change to abundance in time. He expects you to multiply what He has given you.

And you shall remember the LORD your God,
for it is He who gives you power to get
wealth, that He may establish His covenant
which He swore to your fathers, as it is this
day. (Deuteronomy 8:18)

I have traveled to several countries that have very little resources for their people. **In my travels, I noticed the same trend. Those who depend on anything other than Christ were in lack.** It does not have anything to do with money, but lack has everything to do with precedence. What is priority?

Remember the man with the five talents? (about $5,000). Then the man with two talents? (about $2,000). Finally, the one man with one talent? (about $1,000). The first two men were so happy and blessed. They used what they had, and multiplied it. The amount of talents, or money wasn't important. They just wanted to help others, and so they did. The man with one talent was afraid of his lord, or at least that was his excuse. He had a mind-set of hoarding what was given to him. He wasn't going to use his money to help anyone. No one was going to tell him how or what he could do with his talent. Therefore, he buried it. If this man's excuse was legitimate, when his master returned, he still was at fault for thinking wrong. He didn't have knowledge of his Master's ways.

My people are destroyed for lack of knowledge. Because you have rejected knowledge, I also will reject you from being

priest for Me; Because you have forgotten the
law of your God, I also will forget your
children. "The more they increased, the more
they sinned against Me; I will change their
glory into shame.   (Hosea 4:6-7)

Many people in America have little to no
knowledge of the Lord's ways. When something
bad happens, Christ is the first to be blamed. I
have met people in the United States, even in
churches, who refuse the wisdom of God. Some
were wealthy, and others were poor; money is
not the point. Many have a form of godliness.
They know how to talk the talk, but not how to
walk the walk. They are in and out of church.
They blame others, and live in the past. They
live far below the mind of Christ, and for some
reason they just don't get it. They think
everyone else is wrong, and they are right. They
know God's word. However, they live as though
it's just another book. They take bits and pieces
out of scripture and tell it as their gospel. They
lie to themselves.

At the same time, I have met people in other
countries who did not have a penny, but they

were rich in Christ. They were not ashamed. They operated with great joy. The fruit of the Spirit seemed to flow from them. Their life radiated Christ. I like what Paul told the church at Corinth.

> *But this I say: He who sows sparingly will also reap sparingly, and he who sows bountifully will also reap bountifully. So let each one give as he purposes in his heart, not grudgingly or of necessity; for God loves a cheerful giver."* (II Corinthians 9:6-7)

Now if all you have is a penny, but you give that penny knowing it is your entire livelihood, God will bless that. God sees the heart.

Either you love Jesus Christ and you hunger for more of His truth and grace, or you are fooling yourself. Remember, one day you will stand before Christ and be judged by your fruit, and your deeds.

> *Declare His glory among the nations, His wonders among all peoples.* (Psalm 96:3)

What does life hold for you and me? Some

fear that they are entering a time of great instability in the world. The recent economic meltdown has created hardships for many people. Some even say that darker days are still ahead. Is that the whole picture? The problem with these predictions is that these men have forgotten what the Lord promised.

> *Let your character or moral disposition be free from love of money [including greed, avarice, lust, and craving for earthly possessions] and be satisfied with your present [circumstances and with what you have]; for He [God] Himself has said, I will not in any way fail you nor give you up nor leave you without support. [I will] not, [I will] not, [I will] not in any degree leave you helpless nor forsake nor let [you] down (relax My hold on you)! [Assuredly not!]*
>
> (Hebrews 13:5 Amp)

Does that get the point across?

What shall we do as we are facing a meltdown? Look to the Lord. I'll tell you again, Psalm 96 is one of three Psalms that were written because of God's people placing the Ark of God in the tent that was prepared for this

Holy thing. This tent was built in the center of Jerusalem.

God's people sang these words:

Oh, give thanks to the LORD! Call upon His name; make known His deeds among the peoples! Sing to Him, sing psalms to Him; Talk of all His wondrous works! Glory in His holy name; Let the hearts of those rejoice who seek the LORD! Seek the LORD and His strength; seek His face evermore!
(I Chronicles 16:8-11)

Increase always follows joy, and peace of mind. What is increase without those traits?

I have gained a friendship with someone who is high up in the ranks of his profession. I noticed a few weeks ago, he seemed troubled so I asked him what was wrong. He told me he had to lay off around 30% of his employees, and he was cutting everyone's pay around 20%, including his own. I told him, I would be praying for him. A few days later, I saw him again, and I shared that I had received a word from the Lord for him. I also believe this is a word for every person who will receive it. I told him, "Increase is coming!" He looked at me and I said, "Increase is coming."

He said, "You're serious."

I told him, "Yes, if you will expect it, and trust in the Lord. Increase is yours!" Then I gave him a verse that has always ministered to me:

> *If you are willing and obedient, You shall eat the good of the land; But if you refuse and rebel, You shall be devoured by the sword";* *For the mouth of the LORD has spoken.*
> (Isaiah 1:19-20)

That's pretty strong language don't you think? So obedience brings favor.

What state of mind are you living in? Why not believe for increase instead of saying, "Everything is going to fall apart." What you will find is, when others are down you will be joyful in the Lord God.

> *Rejoice in the Lord always. Again I will say, rejoice!* (Philippians 4:4)

Let me point out, in Philippians, you will find the word rejoice or joy, 16 times in just 4 chapters. Remember, when Paul wrote this small book, he was locked away in a prison cell with no windows; It was dark, moldy, and cold. However, Paul's circumstance didn't control him. No, he was living under the mighty hand of God. He knew that his worst day on this earth would become his first day in heaven. Either way, he was not afraid.

For to me, to live is Christ, and to die is gain. But if I live on in the flesh, this will mean fruit from my labor; yet what I shall choose I cannot tell. For I am hard-pressed between the two, having a desire to depart and be with Christ, which is far better. Nevertheless to remain in the flesh is more needful for you."
(Philippians 1:21-24)

Those are the words of a man who is totally sold out for Christ. You will not enjoy life, and its surprises unless you decide to sell out.

And my God shall supply all your need according to His riches in glory by Christ Jesus.   (Philippians 4:19)

Think about that just for a moment, your needs will be met by God's riches through His Son Jesus. I would have to say that you are rich. You are blessed and highly favored.

> *You know the generous grace of our Lord Jesus Christ. Though he was rich, yet for your sakes he became poor, so that by his poverty he could make you rich.*
>
> (II Corinthians 8:9 NLT)

Remember in math when you had to find which number was less than or greater than. Well, Jesus is > sin. Jesus is > sorrow. Jesus is > sickness. Jesus is > any report! Why not have a Selah moment. (That means to pause and think about any situation.) Think, increase is coming. God is all about intensification, and if you follow Him you will experience abundance.

> *Therefore do not worry, saying, 'What shall we eat?' or 'What shall we drink?' or 'What shall we wear?' For after all these things the Gentiles seek. For your heavenly Father knows that you need all these things. But seek first the kingdom of God and His*

righteousness, and all these things shall be added to you. Therefore do not worry about tomorrow, for tomorrow will worry about its own things. Sufficient for the day is its own trouble. (Matthew 6:31-34)

Jesus is saying that open-ended questions aren't good when tied to fear pertaining to food, drink and clothing.

Listen, corporations aren't looking for someone to hire that will ask a bunch of questions. No, corporations look for people with answers to the questions! Jesus Christ is the answer to every question. He says, "Yes I will help; I will change your situation." Jesus is saying, "If you will trust in Me you do not have to worry about *food, water, shelter, or clothing!*" He's saying, "Only Gentiles (pagans) worry," and worry plus faith does not mix. It's like oil and water. It's an oxymoron. Think about verse 32b of Matthew chapter 6 again, "For your heavenly Father knows that you need all these things."

This year, stop pursuing dead issues. Here's three things you need to do concerning dead issues: Admit them, quit them and forget them.

Admit them:

> *If we confess our sins, He is faithful and just to forgive us our sins and to cleanse us from all unrighteousness.*
>
> (I John 1:9)

Quit them:

> *For the wages of sin is death, but the gift of God is eternal life in Christ Jesus our Lord.*
>
> (Romans 6:23)

Forget them:

> *Brethren, I do not count myself to have apprehended; but one thing I do, forgetting those things which are behind and reaching forward to those things which are ahead, I press toward the goal for the prize of the upward call of God in Christ Jesus.*
>
> (Philippians 3:13-14)

Jesus said in Matthew 6:33 *But seek first the kingdom of God and His righteousness, and all these things shall be added to you.*

Suppose someone offered you a tremendous

sum of money, perhaps millions of dollars, but the exact amount would be determined by how well you could learn to speak Spanish in two months' time. You would embark on the most intense crash-course program of learning in your life. You would study from morning to night, burn-the-midnight-oil, listen to language tapes, and carry flash cards. Wherever you went you would seek out fluent Spanish-speaking individuals so you could practice with them. During those two months, no one could drag you near a time-wasting television program. You would probably allow nothing to interfere other than necessary physical activities to sustain life itself. All for money.

Jesus says, seek first, be diligent, love Me, worship Me, and I will bring addition to you. Several years ago, I became very angry because a good friend left me with his big bill. I thought of ways I could get even with him. However one night as I was sleeping I was awakened. I looked at the clock it read 4:44 AM. I went into our living room not knowing the Lord wanted to help me. I picked up the channel changer and as I was about to turn on the television, the Holy Spirit interrupted my plan. My hand began to shake to the point that I dropped the remote control. God then spoke to my heart, "Read Psalm 37." I did. Then He said,"Read it two more times slowly all the way through."

> *Trust in the LORD, and do good; Dwell in the land, and feed on His faithfulness. Delight yourself also in the LORD, And He shall give you the desires of your heart.*
> (Psalms 37:3-4)

As I finished reading Psalm 37 through the third time, I felt a huge weight lifted off of me. I experienced joy that only could come from God. Suddenly my eyes came off of my dilemma, and were open to the Lord's goodness. I was totally delivered from all resentment. Guess what? I paid that debt off in record time. God knew I couldn't be blessed or be a blessing with junk in my heart.

To delight in the Lord means to take pleasure in, desire, be pleased with, have peace with contentment. Every day another 24 hours or 1,440 minutes or 86,400 seconds is credited to your account. How will you spend them?

God desires to give you increase, but can you receive it? Instead of struggling to change what can't be changed, allow God's transforming power to sweep over your life. He can break the ties between you and all those tormenting thoughts of your past. Let them go today in Jesus' name.

I met with a friend in the ministry a while back. I told him how I had made a big mistake earlier with a decision. He looked at me and said these truthful words, **"Howard, you have to let the past go."** He could not have expressed the truth to me any better. That day became a new day for me, and I have never looked back. As you grow in Christ, you will have many testimonies of victory over pain.

While walking with the Lord it's so important to know that He is never shocked by your feelings. Whether good, bad, or indifferent, He can handle them. He is interested in what is going on in your life, and is willing to trade with you. God loves to make deals in order to bring a win-win situation. In Genesis, the Bible tells of Abraham interceding. He asked if God would spare the city if there were 50 righteous inside. Not being sure of how many righteous people, he continued in his deal making. He went on until he got the number down to 10 righteous.

God is a master barterer. He'll give beauty for ashes, a garment of praise for the spirit of heaviness. If there is weeping at night, He'll give joy in the morning. If you're in the path of destruction, He'll bring deliverance.

The Lord says, "Prove me," in bad economic times. His transactions are heavenly, because his currency is divine.

If you have mustard seed faith He has mountain-moving power. He'll use your fearful obedience. You will see an evil army slain.

Take a look at the beatitudes in Matthew chapter 5. The Lord says, "Blessed are the poor in spirit, for they will inherit the kingdom of heaven. Blessed are the mourners, for they will be comforted. Blessed are the meek, or the timid, for they will inherit the earth. Blessed are the hungry, and the thirsty for they will be filled."

Remember the widow who only gave 2 mites. She was rewarded for giving her all. You see, it's not about trading apples for apples. It's not about giving our best for His best.

It's about your worst for His best. Your sin, doubt, and fear for His love, which is perfect. His love is blind. He gets the bad end of the deal in the world's view. He's not a fair trader; he always takes your discarded articles and gives you back priceless, ageless, limitless resources.

The God who loves to make Divine transactions is ready to trade for your garbage. So now you understand why I say you can live in increase. It's because what He *has* is freely given to us, if we are willing to trade!

Questions

Can be answered in a group, or as an individual

Do you have a song within? What kind?

Do you believe in spiritual prosperity?

How are some ways you can refresh your walk with the Lord?

Is the Ark in the center of your life?

What would you like to trade?

129

If you could, what three things would you place in God's ark in order to receive an increase?

1)

2)

3)

How has God allowed you to prosper?

Living In The Moment

When one decides to live life now, and stop procrastinating, that person will find purpose. **The word live as defined in the dictionary says, " to be alive at a specified time." The phrase, "live in the moment" means to live or act without worrying about the future.** What about the past? For some, it is not an issue, they don't have any regrets or worries about the past. For others, the past has paralyzed their ability to live and appreciate each moment. So much in life hinges on how you use your time.

See then that you walk circumspectly, not as fools but as wise, redeeming the time, because the days are evil.Therefore do not be unwise, but understand what the will of the Lord is.
(Ephesians 5:15-17)

Paul tells you to walk carefully. The choices you make in life affect the next minute, hour, day, etc. What should you do then? What if you make the wrong choices? Maybe you should do nothing. Maybe there won't be any bad consequences. Wrong! Have you ever dreaded something so bad you simply put it off to face later? My point is, you need to live life now, stop procrastinating and find purpose. That might sound simple, but as one lives life he or she finds a lot to repair, throw away, and even add.

My wife and I enjoy watching a very popular channel on TV. The channel is all about home improvement and decorating. We get caught up in watching other people as they tackle their projects. The crazy thing is we haven't finished our own tasks. It's more fun to watch others than to champion our own. You laugh at the irony of it, but we also know that we represent a lot of people. What about those cooking shows and fitness shows? Wow, we should all really be inspired by now. However, being a bystander beside the television is easier than actually getting in the game of life and doing, or being something, or somebody?

Also, procrastination occurs when you feel like something is looming over your head. It won't go away by sitting there, either. A feeling of being overwhelmed creeps in, and all the plans to seize the moment are gone. This creates a cycle of dread. Dreams that are not realized can cause depression. When a person just accepts whatever comes without becoming proactive an enemy named "Average" enters.

Hope deferred makes the heart sick, But when the desire comes, it is a tree of life.
(Proverbs 13:12)

The best way to deal with disappointment is through the Word of God and prayer. The reality is, many people will choose a different route to relieve their pain. Notice verse 12 says... *when desire comes, it is a tree of life.* Living in the moment brings desire, passion, and new hunger. I like the fact that I can eat from the tree of life now. No more spoiled stuff.

One of the largest crises in America is the abuse of prescription medicine. Prescription medications are legal and many times are needed to treat legitimate illnesses and chemical imbalances. For many, however, prescribed medicine has become a crutch. People hide and escape behind the temporary effects of medicine. Too often, they find it easier not to live in the now, and to snooze through the difficult times. Some medicines produce a sense of euphoria and speed them into a phony future. It's really sad to think that millions are looking for their next high. Someone who abuses drugs will tell you, they will wait all day for their fix.

> *Moreover the word of the LORD came to Jeremiah a second time, while he was still shut up in the court of the prison, saying, "Thus says the LORD who made it, the LORD who formed it to establish it (the LORD is His name): 'Call unto Me, and I will answer you, and show you great and mighty things, which you do not know."* (Jeremiah 33:1-3)

Though Jeremiah was shut up in bondage, the word of God was not bound. I am so glad God's word can have free course in our lives in any circumstances. You might be bound by chains right now, but God's word is waiting to give you complete release. Jeremiah lived in the moment; therefore, he knew things were bad, but soon exile would end! The Lord promised that the people who keep their hope and faith in God shall again be filled with joy.

> *When the Lord brought back his exiles to Jerusalem, it was like a dream. We were filled with laughter, and we sang for joy. And the other nations said, "What amazing things the Lord has done for them." Yes, the Lord has done amazing things for us.*
> (Psalm 126:1-3 NLT)

Israel dreamed again. They were filled with laughter; they sang with joy. Other nations were touched. They didn't live with regret. Whatever you are facing, if you desire, he can lead your steps. There's nothing worse than living life without a dream.

Again, living in the moment means becoming relevant and real in prayer and through God's word. Many people live with past memories, some live with remorse, and even others live in the future. They use sentences like, "One day I'll get to have my dream, and then I'll be happy." What does tomorrow hold? Jesus Christ is in your moment; He's living real time with you.

God is our refuge and strength, A very present help in trouble. (Psalm 46:1)

A few months ago, I received a nice 3-page brochure from the IRS giving me an estimation of what I will have when I reach 67, or if I choose to work until 70. I was showing it to my wife, and began to think about the worries of not having enough even if I work until 70. The Lord checked me and said, "Are you going to live 30 years in the future and worry, or will you trust Me to take care of you right now?" The enemy hates for a believer to live in the moment with Jesus Christ. When you trust God it frightens the devil because he knows: if God is for you who can be against you?

Living in the moment does not mean you stop thinking about heaven or your loved ones who have gone on before you.

No, you should never forget the past, and by-all-means, you hold on to eternity. However, for you to become relevant at home with your children, spouse, job, and church you have to get in the now. Many people stop living because of grief, hurt, rejection, or physical pain. I have found problems in my body on several occasions each time I decided to take a down-to-business stance. I can't afford to wait around or get others to pray. I wear the whole armor of God. I begin to speak out loud over my affliction. I'll look in the mirror every morning and night and speak wellness over my body. By faith through grace every time God heals my body.

> *Finally, my brethren, be strong in the Lord and in the power of His might.Therefore take up the whole armor of God, that you may be able to withstand in the evil day, and having done all, to stand.* (Ephesians 6:10,13)

This armor should never be placed on the shelf. It should never collect dust, because the devil has his schemes. **The armor of God was**

given to you, so you could win every battle. Christ shed His own blood for your victory! If you are like me, while you are in the middle of some of these battles it seemed as though you lost. In time, looking back, you will see God's hand in everything. Just give it some time. If the Lord tarries His coming, one day you will be healed.

Therefore, I say again, time is all you have. One day, you will have less time than you think. Don't allow time to be wasted. Buy a day planner or whatever it takes. One of the greatest ways to start every day is in prayer. Prayer seems to place everything in its proper order.

Think about this, Jeremiah's peers did not want to hear what he had to say. So they locked away this weeping prophet. What a low blow unto Jeremiah. However, Jeremiah was living in the moment. Jeremiah was God's present spokesman. Again, Judah didn't like his truthful words, because His truth was harsh. He spoke of pain, and change. **Hint: people don't like change.**

Judah wanted to sin, and live any old way. They wanted to worship pagan gods while still having the luxury of fine things. They wanted Jehovah on their terms. How convenient. Even while Judah sinned directly against God, God proclaims whom He will help.

In those days Judah will be saved, And Jerusalem will dwell safely. And this is the name by which she will be called: THE LORD OUR RIGHTEOUSNESS.

(Jeremiah 33:16)

God was willing to trap Judah and capture them for their own good. He hungers for you to be His righteous. He'll do what it takes for this to occur. He's not in the business of hurting people. If that were the case everyone would be destroyed. Many times, God will allow events so He can work out His perfect plan, once again, through you. Regardless of what you think, that's love.

Therefore, I urge you, brothers, in view of God's mercy, to offer your bodies as living sacrifices, holy and pleasing to God—this is

*your spiritual act of worship. Do not conform
any longer to the pattern of this world, but be
transformed by the renewing of your mind.
Then you will be able to test and approve
what God's will is—his good, pleasing and
perfect will.*   (Romans 12:1-2 NLT)

As you keep focus, you will know God's
perfect will. I cannot tell you how many times I
have looked back at points in my life only to see
God's purpose unfold.

*For thus says the LORD: 'David shall never
lack a man to sit on the throne of the house of
Israel;*   (Jeremiah 33:17)

In other words, out of David's lineage will
come the Messiah; there will be no breakage or
loose ends, because "I the LORD will take care
of My people!" God was saying, "Even if I have
to shut them up, and shut them down, I the
Lord will be glorified through them."

As you live in the moment you will begin to
notice God's handiwork time, and time again.
Living in the now keeps you from closing your
eyes and wishing your life away. It will even

help you through struggles you didn't create. You will become too busy for messes. After all, you have a mission to carry out because your plan came from God.

These two chapters in Jeremiah have brought new meaning about God's love for me. Throughout chapter 32 and 33, God proclaims how He loves Judah and the generations to come. He cries out, "I love them with all My heart, and strength." God loved His people through out the Old Testament; moreover, He loves us even now.

> *Ah, Lord GOD! Behold, You have made the heavens and the earth by Your great power and outstretched arm. There is nothing too hard for You.* (Jeremiah 32:17)

Angels spoke these same words to mere men at the conception of Jesus Christ. "Is there anything too hard?" Jesus said similar words to His disciples. Therefore, I ask you, "Is there anything too hard for God?" Nothing has really changed; however, now you have access unto the grace of God. How blessed can a person be.

You have the ability to come boldly unto the throne room of grace at any time. Just as God looked for the righteous then, He looks for the righteous now.

> *For the eyes of the LORD are on the righteous, And His ears are open to their prayers; But the face of the LORD is against those who do evil.* (I Peter 3:12)

Things might be bad, even hopeless. Moreover, your life in the moment (Real Time) seems to have a period at the end. However, just as God took care of Judah, He's going to take care of you. God will have the final say.

> *This is the day the LORD has made; We will rejoice and be glad in it.* (Psalms 118:24)

David and four hundred men who were once lame physically and emotionally came out of the cave of Adullam. They had been trained by their leader, and they were ready for battle. For they have learned to live in the now. They listened and heeded to their leader's voice. Proclaim with me the same words these men declared back then, "This is my day!"

Questions

Can be answered in a group, or as an individual

Do you live in the moment? Why not?

List some areas in your life you desire to change.

Do you live with hurt?

Is there anything keeping you back?

143

Presently, how are you making a difference?

Do you waste time?

List some past pain that you deal with.

How would you like the future to be for you?

List some things you would like to do for others.

Exercise Your Way To Victory

Okay, it's time for a little temple maintenance. After 30 years of running, I think I am qualified to help you with your physical body. I have pounded thousands of miles on streets, sidewalks, and country roads. If I were to average running three times a week, two miles a run, for thirty-one years, it would total around 10,000 miles, and that is a very low estimate. Some day's, especially for the first few years, I ran eight to twelve miles five times a week. So really the miles I ran are a lot higher, maybe somewhere around 16,000 miles. I like to think I'm getting close to running around the world. I sound like I am bragging, and maybe I am. It is a triumph over the flesh, for me.

However, the greatest success in my life will come when I see my Lord face to face.

While I am running, the Lord has my full attention, my mind is totally fixed on Him. I have received wonderful revelation from God in those few moments. Maybe it's because blood is pumping through my body so fast into my heart lungs and brain that my mind is able to be more fine tuned to His voice. He wants us to hear Him so we may exhort others. If you are serving the Lord faithfully, let me be the first to tell you that you have something to share with people. Be a disciple, an encourager and perhaps you too, might want to write a book someday. Those who stay faithful, and keep a great attitude should be honored.

Let him who is taught the word share in all good things with him who teaches.
(Galatians 6:6)

Nowadays, I go to the gym primarily because I have found that a treadmill is easier on my joints. There have been some negative things written about running, but just a few months ago I heard doctors saying that more studies have been done. The studies say those who run daily have better knees and joints than those who do not exercise. I could have told those doctors that. (Just kidding!)

> *Do you not know that those who run in a race all run, but one receives the prize? Run in such a way that you may obtain it. And everyone who competes for the prize is temperate in all things. Now they do it to obtain a perishable crown, but we for an imperishable crown. Therefore I run thus: not with uncertainty. Thus I fight: not as one who beats the air. But I discipline my body and bring it into subjection, lest, when I have preached to others, I myself should become disqualified.* (I Corinthians 9:24-27)

In the book of I Corinthians, Paul relates the believer's life as that of a runner. I can tell you this: the times I wanted to stop running but kept going, I felt as though I broke some kind of barrier. You know as well as I do that the believer's walk is filled with barriers. Remember this, the faithful will obtain a crown that does not fade away. Be a barrier breaker.

> *Don't you see that you can't live however you please, squandering what God paid such a high price for? The physical part of you is not some piece of property belonging to the spiritual part of you. God owns the whole works. So let people see God in and through your body!* (I Corinthians 6: 20 TM)

I'm telling you that it is worth it. Whatever you face, God's grace is bigger, better, and greater. By the way, God's grace is His ability to do in you, what you can't do. God will see you through.

> *For whatever is born of God overcomes the world. And this is the victory that has overcome the world—our faith.*
> (I John 5:4)

If you have faith in Jesus Christ you have victory. Faith has been given to you, so you will win over everything. Your faith allows you to overcome.

Once while running, I stepped into a large hole. It was almost night, and I could not see well. Here's a lesson: "Don't run in the dark!" My first thought was to stop and cry, but then I remembered my dad and mom lived over sixty miles away and by the time they arrived I would be dead of hypothermia. Therefore, I made myself run on, and even as I passed my house I told my ankle, "You will finish this run." Guess what? I did, and the next day my ankle was twice the size as the other one; however, I am convinced if I had given in to the pain while hearing the twist, feeling the ache, and knowing what a deep hole it was. I would probably still be laying there.

The believer's life is not for quitters. Paul told Timothy,

Stay clear of silly stories that get dressed up as religion. Exercise daily in God—no spiritual flabbiness, please! Workouts in the gymnasium are useful, but a disciplined life in God is far more so, making you fit both today and forever. You can count on this. Take it to heart. This is why we've thrown ourselves into this venture so totally. We're banking on the living God, Savior of all men and women, especially believers. (I Timothy 4: 7-9 TM)

The King James version says, "bodily exercise profiteth little." So it's safe to say Paul wasn't putting down exercise. He just made sure everyone knew what was essential. Some of my greatest thoughts about God come as I exercise. I have found that when I am tired or feel drained physically the best thing I can do is exercise. You naturally want to rest when tired, but if you will get up and exercise, you will find new energy. I can't tell you how many times I have felt like sleeping, or doing nothing, but I made myself work out. Remember I Timothy 4:7 says to "exercise yourself toward godliness." It changes the attitude and body and makes the whole day different.

Again, I have days where it seems as though I just can't run, or near the middle of my workout I have wanted to quit. I have never given in to those emotions. I feel as though my workouts are very similar to my personal walk with the Lord. I will not allow my body or my mind to limit me. I will continue on in my journey. Guess what? Every time, I can honestly say I feel better. The same is true in our Spiritual walk.

Sometimes you don't feel like having devotions, but when you stick to the discipline, you will not be sorry. At the beginning of Jesus' ministry, He called twelve disciples. The very name disciple means one who is disciplined. After three and a half years, Peter, James, John and the other nine had not become perfect but they continued. Today, people don't really think about the disciple's failures. They are remembered as giants in the New Testament church. God desires this for you also. He hungers to make you a giant, or maybe a giant killer!

Many times in your walk with the Lord, you'll get hurt because some people just aren't right. I call them living on another level." Maybe a level with the devil. Some folks seem to live just to hurt God's righteous people. You need to get back up and keep running the race because there aren't any options. Sometimes, I think

Christians like to talk about their battle scars. However, healing won't come until you forgive.

> *Don't pick on people, jump on their failures, criticize their faults—unless, of course, you want the same treatment. Don't condemn those who are down; that hardness can boomerang. Be easy on people; you'll find life a lot easier. Give away your life; you'll find life given back, but not merely given back—given back with bonus and blessing. Giving, not getting, is the way. Generosity begets generosity.* (Luke 6:37-38 TM)

So do a little forgiving. Before you know it, you will sense new freedom and liberty.

Once while running in a 10K race, I was coming close to the finish line when I heard a man shouting, "Run, run, you can do it, run!" I knew he wasn't cheering me on because I did not know him. The young man behind me recognized his voice of encouragement, though. Before I could blink an eye, this young man who was behind me, passed me.

What's my point? Everyone needs affirmation. To be honest, as I heard and knew this voice wasn't for me, I felt let down. Maybe I even slowed down physically. You will be surprised what encouragement will do. If you can be sincere, you need to find someone to encourage. Everyone needs a voice of support. Remember, as you give it will be given back to you. Sowing and reaping is a universal law.

> *While the earth remains, seedtime and harvest, cold and heat, winter and summer, And day and night shall not cease.*
> (Genesis 8:22)

Remember, the accolades you are seeking are far superior and eternal than any race!

> *I have fought the good fight, I have finished the race, and I have remained faithful.*
> (I Timothy 4:7)

Paul refers to faithfulness, and eternity as finishing the race. Maybe it's because the temporary struggles of finishing a race are hard work.

As Paul reviewed his life, he used the figures

of a wrestler, a runner, and a soldier. Only God's grace can help you to be a strong finisher in the Christian life.[5]

Just to put some of you at ease, the first time I ran with my brother he was off for a twelve mile run. In my mind I was too, but after five hundred yards my whole body cried out, "No you won't!"

Sometimes I forget to tell about that part of getting started as a runner. Start slow. Pace yourself. It's better to start slow and finish well. God's word declares, do not despise small beginnings. Please, always remember where you have come from. It saddens me when I meet someone that once stopped to say hello, but now he or she can't because they're too busy, or just too big-headed.

In the last year I've tried something new for my health, and that is lifting weights with machines. Using a curling bar, and some dead weights. I have gotten a lot stronger, and I feel so much better. At my age I can feel, and yes even see a change in my body.

I believe that every person should begin to take personal care of their body. Eating right is very important. If you have a bad habit, a little fasting can help you break it. Your stomach will not like this idea, but remember Jesus said some things will not transpire, or change, but by prayer and fasting.

I seem to hear often that young men in their forties are dying of heart attacks. This isn't God's best. Diabetes among teens is rising. We must realize that God created everyone to be active. Please make the change. Refuse to die of overindulgence. Some men have vowed never to drink or smoke because they saw the devastating effects it had on a close relative. That's commendable. However, what if everyone would take a look at men and women who said no to all the right things, but never treated their own bodies with respect. Therefore, they died too early. Most people never think about their physical body being so important, but it is. Many things that make people sick can be reversed.

And so, dear brothers and sisters, I plead with you to give your bodies to God because of all he has done for you. Let them be a living and holy sacrifice—the kind he will find acceptable. This is truly the way to worship him. Don't copy the behavior and customs of this world, but let God transform you into a new person by changing the way you think. Then you will learn to know God's will for you, which is good and pleasing and perfect.
(Romans 12:1-2 NLT)

Many times as your thought process changes your body follows. That's exactly what happened to me. I knew I needed a transformation, but I couldn't change until Christ entered. When He's welcomed everything changes. As you exercise, fellowship with Him. Some of my best times come as I walk or run.

Now all glory to God, who is able, through his mighty power at work within us, to accomplish infinitely more than we might ask or think.
(Ephesians 3:20 NLT)

To begin exercising find a trainer, gym, or doctors office, and discover what your body fat is. Tell the doctor to be totally honest with you. Ask him about your weight and health. Maybe a physical would be a good thing to get done. Write down some goals, get pictures of your vision, and place them in a spot where you will see them daily. Remember, start off slow because you have the rest of your life. Who knows, one day you might become a marathon runner.

So you also should consider yourselves to be dead to the power of sin and alive to God through Christ Jesus. (Romans 6:11 NLT)

No one will appreciate the accomplishments like you. So lift up your head, pull up your Spirit and begin. Winston Churchill once said, "The price of greatness is responsibility."[6]

He gives power to the weak and strength to the powerless. Even youths will become weak and tired, and young men will fall in exhaustion. But those who trust in the Lord will find new strength. They will soar high on wings like eagles. They will run and not grow weary. They will walk and not faint.
(Isaiah 40:29-31 NLT)

Over and over again, throughout God's word your body is called God's temple, so treat it in that regards.

Don't you realize that your body is the temple of the Holy Spirit, who lives in you and was given to you by God? You do not belong to yourself. (I Corinthians 6:19 NLT)

Right now, the very presence of God lives within you. The One who lives within you is far greater than gold or silver. You have the very presence of God living inside, so take care of His temple.

If this word has uplifted, inspired, restored, or convicted you, please refer it to your friends or small groups.

May you be blessed in Jesus name, Amen.

If you do not have a relationship with the Lord Jesus Pray this prayer: Jesus I am a sinner. Please forgive me. I believe that Jesus is the Son Of God and that He died and was raised from the dead and I ask Him to Come into my heart. I renounce the devil. Come, live in me from this day forward. Now I am a new man. Thank you Jesus.

Buy a Bible that is simple to read with a good commentary. Begin reading in the book of Psalms. Stay in the four gospels, and you will grow. Let me encourage you also, to find a good Bible based church and get connected.

Questions

Can be answered in a group, or as an individual

Have you ever wanted to exercise?

What keeps you from starting?

Are you willing to set a time daily to exercise?
What time?

Write down some goals for your physical body.
Clip a picture or two.

Do you think it's important to care for your
body?

How long do you desire to live?

Do you have any aches and pains?

What do you do when you are tired?

Meet the Author

Howard A. Strickland has been in the ministry full-time for twenty years. He's a pastor through and through. He loves people and it shows. His heart leaps for Christ. He desires to see the body of Christ grow! The word of God is his heartthrob and passion.

Presently, Howard is the Senior Pastor of Crane Eater Community Church. Howard is the Captain Chaplain of Gordon County Sheriff's Office. He completed his Doctorate. (from North Carolina College of Theology). He has grown and taken two churches into major building programs with tremendous success.

Pastor Strickland has been humbled by the opportunity to be featured twice on Sermon Central - the world's largest sermon resource center. He has also served on several boards within his denomination. He stays involved in his community through many organizations.

This book was inspired through Howard's personal walk with Christ Jesus. Christ has proven Himself to Howard and his family time and time again. He can't help but write about his Savior. The book is filled with some of the lessons he has learned through experience. As you read this book, it is Howard's hope that you will be inspired and will realize that we are truly His living epistles!

Endnotes

1. http://www.poetseers.org/the_great_poets/ celtic_poems/4 The Lorica of St Patrick

2. Dake's Annotated Reference Bible, John 4,5 Page 9 'J' (Lawrenceville, Georgia 30246)

3. A.W. Tozer, The Knowledge of the Holy Spirt(New York, NY: Walker and Company,

4. http://www.ewordtoday.com/comments/ Classic Bible Commentaries, History's Most Renowned Commentary Writers. Matthew Henry Concise (II Cor. 5:21)

5. 1996 Our Daily Bread, April,18, 2009, Insight, RBC Ministries (Grand Rapids,MI 49501-2222)

6. The Best Of The Word For You Today 2007, Celebration Enterprises (PO Box 5130, Alpharetta, GA. 30023) Dec. 23 The Blame Game.

TEXT MESSAGES FROM GOD

Practical Messages That Touch The Heart

Discover Your Purpose and Assignment For Life!

<u>Great for Small Groups</u>

Purchase this great book at www.amazon.com or <u>www.howardstrickland.com</u> or mail: Howard A. Strickland 612 Shenandoah Drive Calhoun, Ga. 30701 enclose $12.00 it will be shipped.

3593579

Made in the USA